YOUR CREATIVE IDENTITY TRANSFORMATION

For Women Who've Spent a Lifetime Believing "I'm Not Creative"

By

Cindy Wider

Copyright

ISBN: 978-1-7636342-1-3

Published in Australia by StuartCindy Art
First Edition

Email: cindy@drawpj.com
Websites: DrawPj.com | CindyWider.com

Dedication

To the woman who has always shown up as the best version of herself.

Accomplished. Successful. Proud of who she is today.

Yet she knows something's missing.

"I couldn't draw a stick figure to save myself," she says with a laugh.

But deep down, she knows it's true.

This book is for her.

The woman who has achieved remarkable things and is now asking: "I'm sure there's more to me. Something untapped."

She's ready to embrace it and become the true Queen of her rightful destiny.

That calling is creativity.

This book reunites the accomplished analytical woman with the creative self she set aside years ago—not knowing it was even there.

It's time to awaken the spirit from within. The creative self that's ready to finally emerge.

Praising "Your Creative Identity Transformation"

"Never in my wildest dreams did I expect to be illustrating my own children's book, which was a lifetime dream. When I started with you, Cindy, I was unable to draw a circle, an ellipse or anything."
— Mary Egan, Director of Nursing (Retired), Ireland, Age 70

"Cindy changed my life. Not for a year or two, but a lifetime."
— Lyn Donald, Queensland, Australia

"You gave me the confidence to call myself an artist. I learned more in the first two weeks than all the courses I tried."
— Linda Elliott, Corporate Management (Retired), USA

"After studying your course, there was a significant change especially in my attitude to what I am able to learn and achieve, despite my age (now 65). By the way, since I started drawing with Cindy, I enjoy life a lot more."
— Ann Wilson, Age 65

TABLE OF CONTENTS

A Note to Readers

This book shares my personal experience and professional observations from 33 years of working with analytical women to awaken their creative identity through drawing.

While I am a qualified art therapist, this book is intended for educational and inspirational purposes and is not a substitute for professional medical or therapeutic advice.

The stories shared represent individual experiences. Your creative journey will be uniquely your own, and results will vary based on your commitment and practice.

This book is an invitation to explore your creative identity—not a guarantee of specific outcomes, but a proven pathway that has transformed thousands of women's lives.

Introduction

The Question That Changes Everything

There's a question I hear all the time from women. They don't always say it out loud at first. Sometimes it shows up as "I need to find something meaningful" or "There's something missing in my life."

But underneath, the real question is this: "Who am I and who am I becoming?" Not what should I accomplish next. But genuinely—who am I beyond the titles, the achievements, the role everyone depends on me to play?

Perhaps you're asking yourself this question right now. You've spent years—maybe decades—being defined by what you do.

The role that told you who you were, that gave you purpose and meaning and a clear sense of self. And somewhere along the way, you started wondering: is this all there is?

For the first time in a long time, you're asking deeper questions. And in that questioning, an identity question emerges.

A Letter to The Woman Reading This

Dear friend,

I don't know your name yet, but I believe I know why you're here.

You've achieved so much in your lifetime and you're feeling a sense of change in the air. You've built a career, served others, proven yourself capable time and time again.

You've been the one people depended on—the professional, the problem-solver, the one who holds everything together.

You've been so strong for so long and all at a price. You've given out so much of yourself to others and now, you know that something has to change.

Somewhere along the way, something shifted. Maybe it happened gradually. Maybe it was sudden. But at some point, you started asking a question that won't go away:

"Is this all there is?"

Not because what you've accomplished isn't meaningful. It is. But because you sense there's something missing. Something you can't quite name. Something that's been waiting patiently all these years while you were busy being everything that everyone else needed you to be.

You're looking for a new purpose in life and asking "Who am I really? Who do I want to become?"

I've been this person for so long and I really want to find the true me. The me that I once felt as a child when I was happy, free and didn't have a care in the world. I want to know where she is.

There is this quiet longing, and it all sits within a deeply-hidden grief. It's a longing to be creative. To create something with your own mind and hands.

Something tangible that you can see, feel and know that it's completely yours. Your creation.

For decades you've believed that you aren't creative and because that belief has been suppressed, hidden so deeply within you, perhaps you don't even know that longing is there.

You might not have even known that the fundamental skill of drawing is a deeply misunderstood language that you never had a chance to develop as a child. You've tried to fill the void with other activities, keeping busy, staying relevant and needed by others, but nothing quite fulfills you anymore.

"Who am I?" often keeps you awake in the early hours and you desperately want a solution, an answer to this question.

The reason you're asking this question is because right now is the exact perfect time for you to finally make this change in your life.

Now you have the freedom, the time, the heart-space to look deep into yourself. Finally you're ready to give yourself permission to become the fullness of who you truly are.

That can be frightening one day, exciting the next, even confusing and overwhelming. It doesn't have to be. When you discover your lost language of drawing, the carriage that awakens your full creative self, you'll see that you have found your answer to "Who am I?"

This Book Found You

In the depth of your soul you've been crying out for a solution and here it is. The soul knows what it needs to feel fulfilled, happy and complete. The gift of drawing that we are all born with is calling you. It's actually been calling you all of your life but you were too busy, too distracted to notice.

You ignored the calling not because you chose to, it wasn't your fault. It was the demands of society put upon you. You were working hard to hold your life together for those you love and care for and for yourself. That's admirable. You did a great job and should be proud of yourself.

Now the time has come though. You know it. Your soul knows it. It's no accident that you've found this book. This is your guide, to help you move into the next phase of your wonderful life.

The fact is that you are ready. You're ready to move on now, whether you know it or not. Just for the very fact that you picked up this book, that you were curious tells me you've been searching and you're ready. Your entire life up to this point has prepared you for this moment. You're right where you're meant to be.

What I Want You to Know Before You Begin

I'll be with you right by your side every step of the way. There are absolutely no expectations from you. Every woman who comes to me is on her own unique and sacred journey of self-discovery.

When you feel yourself drifting back to old thoughts, insecurities or beliefs that are not serving you on this journey, allow those thoughts to flow through you. Accept them, thank them for caring for you, and tell them that they aren't needed anymore.

When you're in my Creative Identity Transformation™ program, you can write to me about your feelings and thoughts or speak to me 1:1 in a video call. You don't have to perform at any specific level, you don't have to transform into an artist (unless you choose to). This journey is about you finding the fullness of who you truly are through discovering your new creative identity. An identity that says "I absolutely can draw after all." That's huge change.

You don't have to figure this out on your own. I'll be with you every step of the way. When you stumble let me know. I'll be there with kindness, and solutions to help you through.

All you have to do is be willing to let go. Let go of the old thoughts and just open up ready to begin. To be open to the new you. Allow yourself to be free, to be totally you.

We are a partnership, working together as a team to help you discover her...the creative woman within you who you always were and still are.

I've been doing this work for 33 years. I've guided thousands of women through this transformation. And I can tell you this with certainty:

The creative identity you think you lost? It was never gone. It's been preserved inside you all along, waiting for the moment when you finally have space and permission to let it emerge.

That moment is now.

This book is your invitation. Not to become someone different, but to become complete. To integrate the analytical woman you've been with the creative woman you've always been. To answer the identity question with beautiful, undeniable certainty.

I'm honored you're here.

Let's begin.

With warmth and deep respect for the journey you're about to take,

Cindy

Who This Book Is For

I wrote this book for accomplished women from caring and analytical professions—nurses, teachers, healthcare coordinators, administrators, managers, executives—women who have spent their careers being systematic, practical, evidence-based, and focused on others' needs.

Women who believed "I'm not creative. I never was."

Women who are now asking "Who am I beyond my professional role?" and wondering what their creative future could hold.

If that's you, you're in the right place.

What You'll Discover

In this book, I'm going to show you something that might sound impossible right now: that creative capacity you think you never had? It's still there. Unchanged. Preserved. Waiting.
Drawing isn't just a skill. It's a soul language—one you spoke fluently as a child, before you had

to suppress it for survival in a logic-dominated world.

And here's the truth that no one ever told you. You're about to discover that the division between people born as either "analytical people" or "creative people" doesn't exist. It's all a myth. You'll discover why I know this and how your life can change for the better once you see this too.

You're going to discover:

- Why the "analytical vs. creative" divide that's defined your life is a myth
- The part of you that's been missing—and why you didn't even know it was gone
- Why your analytical mind is actually your creative advantage, not your weakness
- How to access your creative capacity on demand—no more waiting, hoping, or wondering if inspiration will show up when you need it
- How drawing becomes the carriage that carries you back to your complete identity
- What happens when the soul language you've suppressed for decades finally has permission to emerge

• The transformation that's possible—from "I can't draw" to holding proof you created yourself
• The quiet power and presence that awakens when you're finally free to be who you were meant to be

This Isn't Just About Learning to Draw

This is about Creative Identity transformation. You'll be transformed from believing "I can't draw" into "Wow! I can draw—look what I created!" You'll be transformed in the way you identify with yourself. You can identify yourself as a creative person and not an "I'm not creative" person. Now you can say "I can draw and therefore I am creative because drawing is creative."

Drawing a realistic self-portrait—one of the most challenging subjects of all time—requires a deep mental shift. You have to go through a process of overcoming the limiting beliefs in your mind.

It's not about the end result you'll be holding in your hand. It's about the journey you went on to get there. The portrait is the evidence, the result.

But under the surface you will have had to focus all of your mind and attention on each angle, size, tone and space to achieve your goal. You will have had to believe in yourself, to trust yourself and show up to actually do the work that was needed.

You'll build the skills yes, but that's only a tiny portion of the journey. You'll also have to overcome any negative beliefs about yourself to draw your portrait. This is a journey in itself.

The realization that you can indeed draw will take your breath away. You'll believe: "Wow! If I can do this, what else can I do?"

Who I Am and Why I Wrote This?

I've been working with analytical women for 33 years, helping them reclaim the creative identity they set aside for decades of service to others.

I'm a multi-award-winning artist, children's book illustrator with 33 years in the art industry, and a qualified art therapist who has transformed the lives of over 22,000 people through internationally recognized courses and transformative programs.

But more importantly, I've witnessed something profound hundreds of times: the moment when a woman who believed "I'm not creative" holds a realistic self-portrait she created with her own hands and realizes everything she thought she knew about herself was incomplete.

That moment of recognition—"I am creative. I always was. What else was I wrong about?"—that's why I do this work.

And that's why I live a very happy life. I love my work. I love serving women, helping them release themselves from their own inner bondages.

I love watching identity expand and witnessing women discover who they're becoming.

What This Book is NOT

This isn't a quick-fix solution or a casual hobby guide. This isn't about staying busy or filling time. This isn't about becoming an artist in the traditional sense (though some of my students do).

This is about identity transformation. About reclaiming a part of yourself that's been waiting patiently for years, perhaps decades.

About answering the question "Who am I now?" with beautiful certainty.

My Promise to You

By the time you finish this book, you'll understand:

• Why you're not "not creative"—you've just never been shown how to access creative capacity you already have
• How your analytical mind positions you perfectly for this transformation
• What becomes possible when you give yourself permission to discover who you're becoming
• The pathway forward, if you choose to take it

This isn't about convincing you to become someone new.

It's about helping you recognize who you've always been.

PART ONE

The Identity Crisis No One Talks About

CHAPTER ONE

Who Am I Now?

For years—maybe decades—you knew exactly who you were.

You were the nurse who held families together through crisis. The teacher who shaped hundreds of young minds. The coordinator who kept entire systems running smoothly. The manager everyone depended on to make things work. The professional who solved problems and made decisions and kept everything functioning.

Your identity was clear, solid, built on years of service and accomplishment.

And then something shifted.

Maybe it's a life transition. Maybe it's reaching a certain age and realizing you want something more. Maybe it's just a quiet voice asking: "Is this all there is?"

And suddenly, there's this space. This beautiful, unfamiliar space where you're asking deeper questions.

Most women try to stay busy. Volunteering. Helping with family. Finding ways to stay useful, productive, needed.

But busyness doesn't answer an identity question.

It just postpones it.

The Pattern I've Witnessed

After 33 years of working with analytical women, I keep seeing the same pattern.

Accomplished professionals—brilliant at what they do. They have capabilities, skills, achievements. They've proven themselves over and over.

And at some point, something shifts.

The initial satisfaction of "I'm good at what I do" starts to feel incomplete. They've done the achieving, the proving, the things they thought would fulfill them.
And underneath all that accomplishment, there's still this quiet question:

"Who am I when I'm not just my professional role?"

What's Actually Missing

Here's what I've discovered: what these women are really missing isn't more achievements or ways to prove themselves.

It's the creative side they left behind years ago.

They just don't know it.

Because they've spent decades—sometimes since childhood—telling themselves "I'm not creative. I never was."

That belief served them during their careers. Their work required systematic thinking, evidence-based decisions, analytical precision. There wasn't room for impractical creative expression when people's health or education or organizational success depended on them.

So creativity went underground.

Not because they weren't creative. But because life demanded something else, and they rose beautifully to meet that demand.

The Loss We Don't Know We're Mourning

It's important to know that we don't even know we're mourning this loss. It's a loss of "permission to create just for the sake of creating." Everything else in our lives is so permission-based. We must work hard at our jobs so that we can succeed so that we can be paid to earn money to survive. We must be a good polite mother, wife, boss, granddaughter, grandparent, auntie, teacher, doctor, nurse to help ourselves and others live in harmony.

There is a loss of personal freedom. Time to just be at one, quietly on our own looking within ourselves. We have given up permission to just create.

The mourning is like a death, it's a deep sadness lost from our lives. With creativity not being expressed we are missing out on a whole beautiful world, a world that can uplift our souls, give us an opportunity to deeply express when words are not enough.

Drawing is the lost language of the soul. It can be used to learn more about ourselves and our worlds. It's not an additional thing for the talented few at all. It's an essential part of our being and as old as creation itself.

When that part of ourselves isn't being expressed, it's like it has been taken away from us. It hasn't. It's still there, but because we aren't using it, we aren't accessing it; just like we discard old items that we believe no longer serve us, then we may as well not have it in our life.

When we lose something (in this case our permission to be creative) then we feel that loss.

Where the "I Can't Draw" Belief Comes From

The number one reason why women believe they can't draw is because they don't know what drawing is or where it comes from. They've completely ruled it out as a possibility even from an age as young as six years.

I've taught many children from all ages and what I know to be true is that drawing is a very significant pursuit in school-aged children. I've seen the shame from young girls hiding their arm across their work when they're not happy with it. I've heard the sadness from children telling me stories about when a teacher dismissed their work as 'ugly' or 'doesn't look like a dog at all' or worse mocks their drawing in front of the entire class.

Drawing is such a deeply intimate experience for a young child and it needs to be acknowledged for the powerful impact it has on a child. It must be respected no matter the perceived quality. It's about a child showing the world her deepest self through her creative output. She shares it to others in a moment of pure innocence, hoping to be admired for what she has created. This is one of the most vulnerable moments in a young child's life. I've heard horrible stories of parents who 'tear up' their child's drawings or remove it from the refrigerator when a child proudly posted it there.

Most of the damage in relation to drawing happens during school age or even before.

When a child is encouraged to draw and shown how to draw their relationship with drawing has a much better chance of survival. The issue is actually far more impactful than we as a society fully grasp. This inability to draw can completely shatter a young child's life before she even has a chance to begin to find her identity.

For many women when the word 'drawing' is mentioned immediately a whole gamut of flashbacks, painful memories and thoughts that were long-hidden begin to appear. These are the very things that she has hidden and suppressed—the pain of rejection, the pain of 'not being good enough' it all started during those very early years when she wanted to draw.

A young child makes up her mind very early on that she can't draw. This is carried entirely through her life.

Drawing should be taught in schools just like Math and English, Science, History and Music. In fact, I did do just that for an entire year as I pilot tested five entire curriculums for years prep to four in a private Christian College. The response was phenomenal, the children truly learned to draw and as a result they carried on the legacy through year levels while they continue to excel with drawing to this day.

Drawing is a perfectly learnable teachable skill but sadly in some schools, there is much less time allowed for learning to draw. There is too little time and too many other more logical pursuits that are given preference. So this myth perpetuates: 'you're either born able to draw or not.'

Until we address this complete fallacy at a root level it will persist all through society. When I show women that drawing is an activity that can be learned just like we learn to play a musical instrument or drive a car, they are amazed to discover that drawing is absolutely within their reach.

The myth about drawing being for the talented few means that very few children grow up believing they can draw and that belief continues into adulthood and beyond.

Along with a belief that they can't draw, these women also believe they are not creative. The correlation between drawing and creativity is that there is a belief that one cannot exist without the other. For example, if I can't draw then I'm not creative.

Many women don't realise at first that creativity comes in many different forms, not limited to drawing. I've chosen drawing as the carriage to lead women into releasing their suppressed creativity. But I also recognize that there are other ways to awaken creativity too.

Creativity is absolutely within every one of us, we just need a fuller understanding of what it is so that we can more easily access it.

It's all around us and expressed in so many ways constantly throughout our daily lives.

The more we educate the world on what creativity truly is and the fact that drawing is not a mystical talent, the more people will believe that they can draw and that they are creative.

I'm on a mission to spread the word and I'm looking for as many other women who will help me to do the same. Together we can share this message with so many other people.

But first, you have to reclaim this for yourself. You have to answer the question that's been quietly waiting.

The Real Question

The real question isn't "what should I do with my time?"

The real question is: "Who am I when I'm not defined by what I do for others?"

And here's what I want you to consider: What if the answer to that question includes discovering the creative identity you set aside years ago?

What if "Who am I?" is actually an invitation to become whole—to bring together the analytical professional you've been with the creative woman who's been waiting inside you all along?

Your Story

Let me guess what your story might sound like. You were probably creative as a child. You drew, you made things, you imagined freely.

And then at some point, maybe in your teens, maybe when you chose your career path, maybe when life demanded practicality, life asked you to be responsible. Focused.

You put away the drawing pencils. You stopped making things "just because." You became who you needed to be to succeed in your chosen field.

And you excelled at it. You were brilliant, accomplished, depended upon.

But that creative part of you? She didn't disappear.

She's been there all along. Patient. Quiet. Preserved.

Waiting for the moment when you finally have space to ask: "What about me? Who am I becoming?"

The Spaciousness

Perhaps you've noticed something beautiful—a quietness, a spaciousness you haven't felt in a long time. Moments when you're not just responding to demands, but actually have room to wonder.

In that beautiful space, a question is emerging: "Who am I now?"

Not what should I do, but genuinely... who am I when I finally have space to discover?

When women create even a little space in their lives, something opens up—this beautiful unfamiliar territory where you can finally wonder and explore and be curious about parts of yourself you set aside all those years.

The Shift I Witness

Here's what I've observed over 33 years: there's a profound difference between "filling time" and "discovering identity."

When a woman is filling time, she finds hobbies. She tries things. Coloring books, knitting, clay, sewing. These activities are lovely—relaxing and enjoyable in the moment. But when she packs them away, the wonder doesn't linger.

But when she stops trying to fill time and starts truly asking "Who am I?"—something completely different happens.

She allows her life to slow down. She begins to live in the moment, to take time to really look, appreciate, and notice her surroundings. She takes time out to "just be" and feels comfortable with solitude. She's not lonely—she admires creation and all of its wonder.

She stops to smell the roses and even more, she begins to notice all the little veins on the petals. She sees a tiny bug and counts the legs. She is in awe, filled with curiosity. Her heart skips a beat and she feels happy.

She looks deeper into herself to find out what makes her happy. What are her likes? Does she like red? What sort of red? Is it an orange-red or a deep cool red? She begins to think about every aspect of who she is. What moves her, makes her feel at peace, what she would like to have more of in her life.

This is the shift—from doing things to pass the time, to discovering who she's becoming.

And in that space, something starts to stir. The creative part of you that's been waiting, patient and preserved and quietly present all along. The part you set aside when life called you toward practicality and responsibility. The part that's whispering now: what if it's my turn? What if there's more to discover?

What If You've Been Creative All Along?

Here's something wonderful I want you to consider—what if "I'm not creative" was never actually true?

You spent your career being observant, detail-oriented, able to see what others missed.

You could assess a situation at a glance, notice patterns, understand how things related to each other in space. You made hundreds of observations every single day.

That's creativity, you know. You just expressed it through nursing, or teaching, or coordinating.

But those same skills—observation, pattern recognition, spatial awareness, attention to detail—they're exactly what drawing is.

You don't lack creative ability. You've just never applied these skills you already have to paper with a pencil in your hand.

What if that's all it takes? What if you've had this capacity all along, just waiting for the right moment to express it in a new way?

Drawing as the Carriage

Here's something I've discovered about this work over all these years—the drawing itself is just the carriage, the vehicle that carries you somewhere beautiful, to discovering who you're becoming.

Because when you sit at your table with a pencil in your hand, something lovely happens. It's your time, completely yours. A quiet space where you're simply being and creating and discovering.

And gently, through practice, you begin to hear a voice you haven't heard in such a long time—your own creative voice, the one that says: I am creative. I always was. Look what I can do.

When Things Come Together

What happens during this transformation is something quite beautiful to witness. You begin gently with loose marks and expressive movements, permission to explore and play without any pressure at all.

Then gradually, structure arrives—systematic techniques, clear steps, building blocks that make perfect sense to your analytical mind.

And somewhere in that process, something remarkable occurs. The creative spirit and the analytical mind—they meet and begin working together in this beautiful harmony. Those observational skills you developed over years become your drawing foundation.

The attention to detail that made you excellent at your work becomes artistic precision.

The systematic thinking that served you throughout your career becomes your pathway to mastery.

You realize: I'm not just making marks. I'm creating something beautiful, something real, something that's coming from me.

The Moment of Recognition

There comes a moment in this journey, and it's different for every woman but it always comes—the moment when you look at something you've created and think: I created this. I actually did this.

That's when everything shifts. Not because you became something new, but because you recognized what was always there.

You have proof now, beautiful tangible proof created by your own hands.

And suddenly the answer to "Who am I?" expands in the most wonderful way.

I am an artist. I am creative. This was here all along.

Not a hobby.

Not just something to fill time. But an identity. A discovery. A homecoming to a part of yourself that's been patiently waiting.

Your Turn

For years—maybe your whole career—you facilitated other people's success and growth. You were brilliant at what you did—the executive who drove strategy, the CEO who led transformation, the manager who solved complex problems, the director who built teams, the coordinator who made everything flow, the nurse who brought calm, the teacher who unlocked potential. You helped so many people discover their own capacities.

And now? It's your turn to discover yours.

Your turn to create and explore and prove to yourself that this creative capacity was always there, just waiting, patient and preserved, ready for exactly this moment when you finally have space to say: yes, now, me.

The Invitation

This identity crisis you're experiencing? It's not a problem to solve.

It's an invitation.

An invitation to discover who you are when all the roles are complete.

An invitation to become whole—analytical and creative, systematic and expressive, both everything you've been and everything you're capable of becoming.

Perhaps the answer to "Who am I now?" is found in curiosity, in the gentle stroke of charcoal on paper, in the quiet discovery that you've always had this capacity within you.

In the beautiful realization that your analytical mind and creative spirit were never opposites at all—they were always meant to work together. And when they finally do? You don't become someone new.

You discover who you've always been—complete, creative, capable of beautiful things.

CHAPTER TWO

What's Been Dormant Inside You All Along

Let me tell you something that might sound impossible right now.

That creative capacity you think you never had?

It's still there.

Unchanged. Preserved. Waiting.

The Difference Between Dormant and Dead

When I tell women their creative capacity is dormant, they often look at me skeptically.

"Cindy, I haven't drawn anything since I was eight years old. How can something be 'still there' after sixty years?"

Here's what I've learned: dormant doesn't mean dead.

Dormant means inactive. Sleeping. Preserved in time, waiting for the right conditions to re-emerge.

Think of it like a seed. A seed can sit dormant for years, even decades, in conditions that don't support growth.

But it hasn't died. Its capacity to grow, to bloom, to become what it was designed to be—that's all still there, encoded in its very structure.

It's just waiting for the right soil, the right light, the right moment.

That's what's happened to your creative capacity.

What Happened in Childhood

Most of the women I work with were creative as children.

They drew. They made things. They imagined whole worlds into existence without questioning whether they were "good at it" or "talented enough."

They just created because creating felt natural.

And then something shifted.

Maybe it was a teacher who said "That doesn't look right." Maybe it was a parent who redirected them toward "practical" pursuits.

Maybe it was just the gradual realization that the world valued analytical thinking over creative expression.

Whatever the moment, they learned: creativity isn't for me. I'm not good at it.

I should focus on things I'm actually capable of.

And so they did.

They focused on math, on science, on systematic thinking. They chose careers that required logic, precision, evidence-based decision-making.

And they excelled.

But the creative capacity? It didn't disappear when they stopped using it.

It went dormant.

The Years of Preservation

For years—maybe decades—you operated primarily from your analytical mind.

You had to. Your work required it. Your patients, your students, your organization, your team depended on your ability to think systematically, make evidence-based decisions, pay attention to critical details.

There wasn't room for both. So creativity was set aside. But here's the beautiful truth: when something goes dormant, it gets preserved exactly as it was.

That creative capacity you had as a child—the ability to see the world with fresh eyes, to imagine possibilities, to express what words can't capture—it hasn't aged. It hasn't diminished. It hasn't been damaged by years of analytical work.

It's been waiting.

Patient. Quiet. Completely intact. Waiting for the moment when you finally have space and permission to welcome it back.

The Conditions for Re-Emergence

So what does dormant creativity need to re-emerge?

When I work with analytical women, they often say: "I should have done this when I was younger. I've wasted so much time. Maybe it's too late now."

But after working with thousands of women for more than 33 years, I've observed something different: creative learning requires specific conditions that many women don't have access to until they create intentional space in their lives.

Not despite your age or life stage. Because you're choosing to prioritize it now.

Four Conditions That Encourage Creative Awakening

When you create space for creative development, four conditions become possible that may never have existed together in your life before. Understanding these helps you see why now can be optimal, not overdue.

Condition One: Claiming Time

What you may have had before: Fragmented time. Stolen hours. Moments squeezed between obligations. "Spare time" that was never really spare. Those little blocks of time—what I call "Pyjama Time™"—that you fritter away because you don't believe you deserve more. (This is why I named my platform DrawPj.com—because we often do our most creative work in those quiet Pyjama moments, before the day's demands take over or after everyone else has gone to bed.)

What becomes possible when you prioritize yourself: Deep, uninterrupted blocks of time that you claim and protect.

Here's the shift: You've become more settled. You know now that you deserve larger blocks of time for yourself. Time to invest in your well-being. You've learned to put yourself first.

You know that if you don't claim that special "me time," no one else will create it for you.

And you understand something profound: self-nurture allows you to truly develop skills in a way that's much harder with smaller interrupted intervals.

Yes, you can learn to draw in those little Pyjama Time™ blocks—I've been saying for years that we don't have to wait for perfect conditions to begin. Small moments add up.

But sustained, uninterrupted time? That's when transformation accelerates.

Learning to draw deeply requires sustained focus—the kind where you can work for two hours without interruption, then return the next day and pick up exactly where you left off.

That kind of continuity accelerates learning exponentially.

When you're not constantly context-switching between work demands, family needs, and personal development, your brain can build skills more efficiently.

The "starting over" every session disappears. Progress compounds.

This isn't a luxury. It's self-investment. And you've reached the point where you know you're worth it.

Condition Two: External Validation

What you may have had before: Everything you did needed to justify itself.

Your boss needed to see results. Your family needed you to be practical. Your community expected you to be responsible.

Every hour spent on yourself required defending.

What becomes possible: Freedom to pursue something simply because it interests you.

No justification needed. No ROI required. No one asking "but what's the point?"

This psychological shift is profound.

When you're not performing for approval, you can focus on genuine skill development instead of impressive-looking results. You can spend time on basic exercises without feeling guilty.

You can "waste time" (which isn't waste at all) exploring techniques that fascinate you. You can be a beginner without shame.

Condition Three: Visual Literacy

What you had at 25: Raw potential. Some technical facility. Limited life experience.

What you have now: Decades of observing the world.

You've watched thousands of faces express emotion.

You've seen how light changes throughout the day across seasons and years. You've observed body language in countless situations.

You've noticed how spaces feel—the weight of objects, the balance of rooms, the rhythm of compositions.

You've accumulated what artists call "visual library"—an enormous collection of observed information that your brain can reference.

Young artists have to build this library while also learning technique. You already have it.

You just need to learn how to access it consciously.

Condition Four: Cognitive Maturity

What you had at 25: Learning ability paired with impatience. Quick uptake but poor persistence. Easily frustrated by slow progress.

What you have now: Mature learning strategies. Realistic expectations. Hard-won patience.

You know from experience that skills develop gradually. You're not expecting to be excellent immediately. You've mastered difficult things before—professional skills, complex projects, challenging situations.

You understand that frustration is temporary and progress is cumulative. This cognitive maturity is worth more than the faster neural processing of youth.

The Convergence Effect

Here's what makes this moment uniquely powerful: It's not just that you can access these four conditions. It's that when you choose to prioritize creative development, all four can exist simultaneously.

In your 20s, you had processing speed and potential, but no time or freedom.

In your 30s and 40s, you had growing expertise, but crushing obligations.

In your 50s, you had skill and some flexibility, but still significant responsibilities.

When you intentionally create space for this work, all four elements can exist together: Time + Freedom + Experience + Maturity = Optimal Learning Conditions.

This convergence is rare. And it's powerful.

What Your Career Gave You

If you were a CEO or executive, you spent years making strategic assessments.

You were seeing patterns in market data, synthesizing complex information quickly, making critical decisions under pressure, understanding spatial relationships in organizational structures.

If you were a business leader or manager, you developed the ability to assess proportions and relationships—budgets, resources, team dynamics—comparing variables, recognizing when something was "off," adjusting systems until they worked.

If you were a nurse, you spent decades making rapid visual assessments, noticing subtle changes, seeing patterns in complex information, working systematically under pressure.

If you were a teacher, you spent years breaking complex skills into learnable steps, recognizing individual learning patterns, adjusting methods when something wasn't working, persistent problem-solving.

If you were a coordinator, you developed systems thinking, multi-variable analysis, attention to detail, long-term project management.

Every single one of these skills transfers directly to learning drawing.

Your career wasn't time away from creative development. It was preparation for it.

Here's what makes this especially powerful for analytical minds:

When you engage your logical brain in the creative process—when you ask it questions like "Which angle is steeper?" or "How do these proportions compare?"—something remarkable happens.

Your logical brain gets a dopamine hit. It's thrilled to be needed, wanted, included in something you're creating.

And that changes everything.

Because now creativity isn't something you wait for. It's not elusive or unpredictable. It's not about hoping inspiration will strike at the exact moment you sit down to draw.

It's accessible. Reliable. On demand.

This is the game-changer: you no longer have to wonder if your creative capacity will show up when you need it. When you engage your analytical mind, creativity becomes trustworthy—something you can count on every single time you choose to create.

For women who have spent their careers being systematic and dependable, this matters profoundly. You don't want to hope. You want to know.

And with this approach, you can.

The Right Pathway

But having these four conditions isn't quite enough. Dormant creativity also needs a systematic, methodical pathway to re-emerge. You can't just decide to "be creative" and have it magically appear.

You need structure, guidance, a framework that makes sense to your analytical mind.

And this is where most women get stuck.

They have the space. They might even have a tiny bit of permission ("Maybe I could try..."). But they don't have the pathway.

They try hobby classes that tell them to "just express yourself" or "follow your intuition"—and their analytical minds rebel because that's not how they learn.

They need systematic instruction. Clear progression. Evidence that they're actually making progress.

They need what I call "the carriage"—a vehicle that carries them from dormancy to creative expression in a way that honors how their minds actually work.

Mary's Story

Let me tell you about Mary Egan.

Mary was a Director of Nursing in Ireland. She retired at 70, having spent her entire career in systematic, analytical, life-or-death decision-making.

When she came to me, she said something I hear all the time: "I can't draw a circle, an ellipse, or anything."

She believed creativity was for other people. She believed at 70, it was far too late.

But I could see what she couldn't: that her observational skills, her attention to detail, her systematic thinking—all the capacities she'd developed over decades of nursing—those were exactly what she needed to draw.

She just needed the right pathway.

Over a short amount of time under my guidance, before she knew it, she was illustrating her own children's book.

Not because she became someone new. But because what was dormant finally had the right conditions to re-emerge.

She told me later: "Never in my wildest dreams did I expect to be illustrating my own children's book, which was a lifetime dream."

A lifetime dream. Dormant for seventy years.

And it was still there, waiting for the right moment.

What's Waiting in You

So what's waiting in you? Not just the ability to draw, though you'll discover that too.

But something deeper. The soul language you had to suppress to survive. The part of yourself that's been missing—the creative, expressive, wonder-filled woman who had to hide so the analytical, systematic, professional woman could excel.

The integration of analytical and creative that you've never experienced—your whole mind working together for the first time in decades.

The answer to "Who am I?" that includes: I am both systematic and expressive, both the accomplished professional I've been and the creative woman I'm finally free to become.

That's what's been dormant. And it's still there, right now, inside you.

Unchanged. Preserved. Waiting for you to create the right conditions for it to emerge. Waiting for you to awaken the soul language that completes you.

CHAPTER THREE

The "I'm Not Creative" Belief

"I'm not creative. I never was."

I've heard this sentence hundreds of times.

From brilliant nurses. Accomplished teachers. Successful coordinators.

Women who spent decades excelling in their chosen fields.

And every single time, they believe it completely.

But here's what I know after 33 years: that belief has never been true.

Not when they first told themselves that story.

Not during the years they carried it. And certainly not now.

Where the Belief Came From

Let's go back to the moment this belief was born.

For most women, it happened somewhere between childhood and early career.

Maybe you drew a picture in school and someone said "That doesn't look right." Maybe you compared your work to someone else's and decided theirs was better, so you must not be talented.

Maybe you simply noticed that the world rewarded analytical thinking with grades, jobs, success—and creative expression seemed impractical, unnecessary, frivolous.

Maybe a well-meaning teacher told you: "You're left-brained, not right-brained. You're good at math and science, not art."

And you believed them. Because they were the authority. Because it seemed to explain why drawing felt hard while analysis felt natural.

But here's what I've discovered after working with thousands of analytical women: that entire divide between "analytical" and "creative" doesn't serve you.

You weren't born on one side or the other.

You were born with both. Analytical AND creative. Systematic AND expressive.

Whatever the specific moment, you made a decision based on false information: I'm not creative. That's not who I am.

And then you spent years collecting evidence to support that belief. Every time you chose logic over intuition, you told yourself: "See? I'm analytical, not creative."

Every time your career required systematic thinking, you reinforced: "This is what I'm good at. Creativity is for other people."

Every time you set aside an urge to draw or make something because you had "more important things to do," you confirmed: "I don't have time for that anyway. I'm not creative."

The belief became a self-fulfilling prophecy. Not because it was true. But because you structured your entire life around it.

What "Creative" Actually Means

Here's the problem: you've been using the wrong definition of creative.

When you say "I'm not creative," what you actually mean is:

"I'm not an artist who can paint like Monet."
"I'm not someone who can draw effortlessly without instruction."

"I don't have some mysterious 'talent' that makes creativity easy."

But that's not what creative means. Creative means: capable of creating.

That's it.

Can you observe the world around you? Can you notice details? Can you assess relationships between shapes, tones, proportions?

Then you're creative. You've just been applying those creative capacities to nursing, teaching, coordinating—not to drawing.

The Artist's Language

Drawing isn't magic. It's not talent. It's not something you're born with or without.
Drawing is a language.

Just like any language, it has vocabulary (lines, shapes, values, proportions). It has grammar (composition, perspective, relationships). It has pronunciation (technique, mark-making, control).

And just like any language, you can learn it if someone teaches you systematically.

You learned English as a child not because you had "talent for language" but because you were immersed in it, taught it step by step, practiced it until it became natural.

Drawing is exactly the same.

The only difference? No one ever taught you the language of drawing in a systematic way that made sense to your analytical mind.

So you assumed you "couldn't do it." But you never couldn't. You just hadn't been taught yet.

What You've Been Calling "Not Creative"

Let me show you something.

Think about your professional career for a moment.

As a nurse, you assessed patients at a glance—noticing subtle changes in color, proportion, spatial relationships. You saw what others missed.

As a teacher, you observed children's expressions, body language, the relationship between their verbal and non-verbal communication. You noticed patterns.

As a coordinator, you visualized how systems fit together, how processes related to each other spatially and temporally. You understood complex relationships.

That's drawing.

Every single one of those capacities—observation, proportion, spatial relationships, pattern recognition—those are the fundamental skills of drawing.

You've been using them your entire career.

You just never called them "creative" because you were applying them to analytical work.

You've been using these four fundamental comparison skills—angles, tones, proportions, and spaces—in your everyday life when you straighten a picture on the wall, tell the time of day just by the tone in the sky, cut a chocolate cake in half and halves again, and arrange the furniture in the home you live in.

These are the exact same skills you need to draw.

The Belief That Served You

Here's what I want you to understand: the "I'm not creative" belief served you beautifully.

It allowed you to focus completely on your career without distraction. It protected you from the vulnerability of trying something you weren't immediately good at. It kept you safe in the systematic, analytical world where you excelled.

In a logic-dominated world that valued productivity, measurable outcomes, and material success, creative expression didn't serve you. Survival meant suppressing that side of yourself in favor of what was practical, profitable, and productive.

Beating to your own drum wasn't safe when analytical precision was valued above all else.

That belief wasn't wrong when you adopted it. It was protective. Necessary for survival, even.

But when you have space and freedom to explore? That same belief can prevent you from experiencing wholeness.

Because the truth is: you are both analytical AND creative.

You always have been. You just emphasized one side for decades while the other waited patiently. And now? You're finally safe. Finally free to explore who you never had a chance to be.

The Evidence Against Your Belief

What if I could show you undeniable evidence that you are creative?
Not through words or theory, but through something you create with your own hands?

That's what happens through the Creative Identity Transformation™ methodology.

Women who believe "I can't draw a stick figure" complete realistic self-portraits that look exactly like them. Not because they suddenly became creative.

But because they always were, and they finally had systematic instruction that awakened the soul language they'd suppressed for survival.

Linda Elliott told me: "You gave me the confidence to call myself an artist. I learned more in the first two weeks than all the courses I tried."

What changed in two weeks wasn't Linda's capacity. It was her belief. And when the belief shifts, everything shifts.

What Becomes Possible

Imagine for a moment that you've been wrong about yourself for years.
Not wrong in a shameful way. But wrong in the sense of incomplete. You thought you were only analytical. Only systematic. Only practical.

What if you're also creative, expressive, capable of beauty?

What becomes possible when you stop telling yourself "I'm not creative" and start asking "What if I am?"

Who do you become when you integrate both sides—the professional you've been and the creative woman you're discovering?

That's not just about learning to draw.

That's about answering the question "Who am I now?" with a completely different answer than you expected.

PART TWO

The Analytical Advantage

CHAPTER FOUR

Your Superpower

There's a myth that won't die: analytical people can't be creative.

It's a false belief that's been perpetuated by society, by every person who said "you're either left-brained or right-brained."

It's a false divide that's kept millions of brilliant women from discovering their complete capacity.

And I've spent 33 years proving that myth wrong.

Now, I want to be clear: I have deep respect for the pioneering work in right-brain drawing theory. It opened doors for millions of people and brought drawing instruction into the modern era.

But my research over three decades has shown me something different—or perhaps, something more complete.

This theory suggested that the logical left brain must become "confused and blocked by the unfamiliar image" and essentially turn off, allowing the right brain to take over the task of drawing.

But that's not what I've witnessed in thousands of analytical women.

What I've discovered is this: drawing doesn't happen because one side of the brain shuts off and the other takes over.

Drawing happens because of the perfect synergy between both hemispheres—the logical analytical brain and the creative expressive brain working together in beautiful cooperation.

The analytical left brain isn't confused or blocked. It's actively engaged—measuring sizes, comparing angles, assessing tones and proportions. It's doing what it does brilliantly: systematic observation and precise comparison.

And the creative right brain? It's finally at peace because it can express itself through making the lines and markings. It loves the beauty of art and drawing.

Both sides. Working together. Integrated. Whole.

This is why analytical women don't need to shut off their systematic thinking to draw. They need to apply it TO drawing.

That's the missing piece. That's what changes everything.

Because here's what I've discovered: your analytical mind isn't your creative weakness. It's your creative superpower.

The Myth of the Artistic Type

Somewhere along the way, we created this false division:

On one side: the artists. Intuitive, emotional, spontaneous, "naturally talented." They create from some mysterious inner wellspring of creativity that can't be explained or taught.

On the other side: the analysts. Logical, systematic, practical, "not creative." They think in structures and patterns, which somehow makes them incapable of artistic expression.

And you've spent your life on the "analyst" side, believing you could never cross over.

Believing the myth. Living inside the lie.

But that division? It's completely false.

It's a construct. A story. A limiting belief that's robbed you of half your identity for decades.

And I'm about to dismantle it completely.

A Common Story

Margaret loved art at 25. Her apartment was filled with half-finished paintings and supplies. Then she enrolled in nursing school.

She made a quiet decision: "I need to be practical now. Creativity is a luxury I can't afford."

She packed up her art supplies, stored them in a closet, and focused on becoming an excellent nurse. Which she did, for 38 years.

But she never touched those supplies again.

When she retired at 63, she felt disoriented. The identity that had defined her for decades was gone.

In its place: "Who am I now?"

While sorting through unused belongings and clearing out her closet one day, she found those old supplies. In a large worn cardboard box. Still sitting, untouched for 38 years. She knew it was there but never truly wanted to throw it away.

She felt something unexpected: yearning.

"What if I tried again? What if it's not too late?"*

I hear this story, or versions of it, constantly. The details change, but the pattern stays consistent:

- Analytical professional
- Practical career choice
- Creativity set aside
- A life transition arrives—retirement, health scare, empty nest, career pivot, hitting a milestone age, reaching the top and wondering "what's next?"
- The question emerges: "What if?"

Why Traditional Art Instruction Challenges Analytical Learners

Here's what typically happens when analytical women try art classes:

The instructor says: "Don't think so much. Just feel it. Loosen up. Trust your intuition. Let it flow."

The analytical student thinks: "I don't understand what that means. How do I 'just feel it'? What does 'loose' look like? Where do I begin?"

When that doesn't work, she's told: "Look, just look. Stare for a while... don't worry, it will come to you. Just keep trying."

She leaves feeling inadequate, her belief confirmed: "See? I'm not creative. This isn't for me."

But here's the real issue: the instruction method didn't match how her brain processes information.

The problem wasn't her capability.

Analytical minds don't respond well to vague encouragement. They need:

- Systematic frameworks
- Logical processes
- Clear methodology
- Step-by-step progression
- Measurable milestones

When I explain to an analytical woman that drawing is pattern recognition, spatial assessment, and comparative measurement, something shifts.

"Wait," she says. "Those are skills I already have." Exactly.

The Creative Skills You Already Use Daily

You're using drawing-related skills constantly without realizing it:

When you straighten a picture frame, you're assessing spatial relationships and angles.

When you portion food equally, you're measuring comparative proportions.

When you arrange furniture, you're evaluating balance, spacing, and visual weight.

When you know the time by looking at the light, you're reading tonal values and atmospheric perspective.

When you coordinate your outfit, you're understanding color relationships.

When you interpret body language, you're making detailed observations and comparative assessments. These are drawing fundamentals.

You've been practicing them unconsciously for decades. Drawing simply teaches you to apply them consciously to paper.

Your analytical mind has been processing visual information all along. You just haven't been shown how to channel it into drawing.

What Analytical Actually Means

Let's talk about what your analytical mind actually does. When you were nursing, you assessed patients systematically. You observed changes, measured vital signs, recognized patterns, made evidence-based decisions.

When you were teaching, you broke complex concepts into step-by-step progressions. You created systematic frameworks. You assessed relationships between ideas.

When you were coordinating, you visualized how systems fit together. You understood spatial and temporal relationships. You organized complexity into clarity.

All of that required:

- Observation (seeing what's actually there)
- Comparison (assessing relationships between elements)
- Pattern recognition (understanding how things fit together)
- Systematic progression (breaking complexity into manageable steps)
- Precision (attention to detail)

Now let me tell you what drawing requires:
- Observation (seeing what's actually there)
- Comparison (assessing relationships between shapes, tones, proportions)

• Pattern recognition (understanding how elements create a whole)
• Systematic progression (building skills step by step)
• Precision (attention to accurate representation)

Do you see it?

The capacities you developed over years of analytical work are exactly—EXACTLY—the capacities you need to draw.

Why Systematic Thinkers Excel

Here's what happens when I work with analytical women:

They excel. Fast.

Not because they're somehow "special" or "talented." But because their minds are perfectly structured for the systematic methodology I teach.

When I say "This line is tilting up, it's on an angle. It's not horizontal. Compare it to horizontal.

How much is it tilting—just a bit? A lot? Or is it nearly horizontal? What direction is the curve tilting towards? Towards the door or the bookcase?" their analytical minds light up.

We don't say left or right because that ignites a more dominant logical brain. We don't want the logical to dominate—we want synergy, to give the creative brain a chance to also have a say, to be involved.

The creative brain is curious, it's the one asking the questions, and the logic loves to answer. Perfect.

When we ask the logical brain a question, it immediately becomes involved. The response is a dopamine high, a thrill. It's so happy to be needed, wanted, and included.

This is a far more reliable way of drawing.

This exact moment allows us to access drawing on demand.

That's profound. That's a complete game-changer.

No longer do we have to hope, wait, and wonder if our elusive creative brain will choose to be present in the exact moment we need it to. At last we can rely on our creativity to kick in the moment we choose to sit at our table to draw.

When the logical brain is involved, the whole process of drawing changes into an incredible power that is accessible, reliable, trustworthy.

This is so important and needs to be fully understood.

They understand immediately. Because they've spent years making exactly these kinds of precise comparisons and assessments.

When I say "Let's break this complex face into simple geometric shapes first, then add detail progressively," they feel relief.

Because that's exactly how they learned everything else in their careers—through systematic, step-by-step progression.

Your analytical mind doesn't prevent you from drawing.

It positions you perfectly for it.

Your Analytical Skills Are Drawing Skills

Let me show you something that will change how you see yourself.

Your analytical work required four fundamental comparison skills that you used every single day:

- The Comparison of Angles - noticing when something was tilted, upright, or off-balance
- The Comparison of Sizes - understanding size relationships between elements
- The Comparison of Tones - seeing differences in light and dark, shadows and highlights
- The Comparison of Spaces - visualizing how things fit together in space

You developed these skills over years of professional work.

You used them hundreds of times every day without thinking about it.

Here's what you need to know: these four comparison skills aren't just nursing or teaching or coordinating skills. They're not just executive decision-making or corporate strategy skills.

They're the exact foundation of drawing.

Every single one of them.

When I teach you to draw, I'm not teaching you new capacities.

I'm showing you how to apply skills you already have—skills you've been using your entire career—to paper with a pencil in your hand.

You already see angles. You already compare proportions. You already notice tone. You already understand space.

You just haven't consciously applied these skills to drawing yet.

Why is it important to translate these skills to drawing? Because that's how drawing becomes the carriage to awaken your creativity.

It provides a very real and physical opportunity for the logical and creative brain to work together.

In this way we can see drawing as a valuable exercise for awakening creativity.

Imagine if we choose to draw for just 30 to 60 minutes before our work day begins (or longer if you're enjoying retirement).

Through including a small amount of time in proper drawing practice (not just random doodles) we not only feed ourselves with a wonderful dose of dopamine, we awaken the dual brain ready for a powerful day.

We position ourselves perfectly for whatever comes before us.

We feel alert, energized, and balanced.

Happy. Content.

And as a bonus, because we've already self-nurtured we appear more calm, serene, peaceful, and magnetic.

(We'll explore exactly how each of these skills translates to drawing in Chapter 6. For now, just know: you already have what you need.)

Why "Follow Your Intuition" Doesn't Work for You

Now you understand why those casual art classes frustrated you.

The instructor said: "Just express yourself! Follow your intuition! Let the creativity flow!"

And your analytical mind shut down completely. And if you've ever had some time with drawing therapy, you felt a need to express yourself more deeply.

Sometimes it isn't enough for you to just "draw" whatever you possibly can, from your heart or feelings, to trust whatever comes out of you. And that's okay.

You need to go deeper, to express yourself on a different level. Your drawings need to at least resemble what you're imagining them to be.

Yes, certainly, other forms of drawing help you express yourself in a different way, Art Therapy is incredibly life-changing and it can help you to process hidden trauma, relationships, explore your deep inner feelings and heal on all kinds of levels and more.

Other forms of drawing including colouring-in and 'Sip and Paint' Parties (such fabulous fun) or paint-by-numbers for example, all help you to relax, feel lovely or peaceful in the moment.

But they don't help you truly change your beliefs about creativity.

Yes, you can heal and yes feel "good in the moment," but your creative identity remains the same afterwards.

Because you don't learn through vague, intuitive exploration. You learn through systematic, clear, step-by-step instruction that builds logically on previous skills.

You need to understand why you're doing something, how it works, what principle underlies the technique. You like to see measurable results. You need evidence-based progression, not mysterious "artistic feeling."

And that's not a weakness. That's your strength.

When you couldn't draw, the problem was never you. The problem was teaching methods that haven't provided for how your mind actually works.

The Systematic Pathway

This is why my Creative Identity Transformation™ methodology works so powerfully for analytical women.

I don't ask you to "follow your intuition."

I teach you systematic frameworks:

"This line is tilting. Compare it to horizontal. Is it tilting just a bit or a lot? Which direction—towards the window or the wall?"

"This tone should be darker than that tone. Compare. See the relationship. How much darker? Translate it to paper."

"This proportion—compare the width of this to the width of that. Are they equal? Is one twice as big?"

Your analytical mind understands this language completely.

Because it's the same language you've been speaking your entire career—observation, comparison, assessment.

And the creative brain? It's finally invited to participate. To express. To make the marks while the analytical brain guides with precision.

The creative brain is given the full depth of release once this process is fully integrated. It takes a certain specific kind of practice to develop the brain pathways needed for the hand to respond to the messages of the analytical mind.

I'm not a neuroscientist and don't claim to understand brain pathway development but there are enough good books available today that tell us how brains can grow and change at any age.

However, it doesn't take long at all to develop this brain hand connection with the right drawing exercises.

Exercises need to be designed specifically in a way that's needed for this interaction to take place.

In other words, when we're refining the comparison of angles, then the exercise needs to focus on that comparison skill specifically.

The result of fully refining the four major comparison skills is the ability to just "draw without thinking."

Drawing becomes a natural skill like riding a bike, driving a car, knitting, playing a musical instrument.

Once this integration has become a natural process, then our deep subconscious can slowly be revealed. Released.

How? Because we have control over what we choose to draw. We don't have to say "I can't draw X because I don't know how."

Instead, we use our drawing fundamentals combined with our Artist's Language and set about using process to create the foundations of our artwork.

Ater that, that’s when the real change happens.

Then we allow the spiritual, emotional feelings to also come into our work. At last we are creating images from our soul on a deep level. We can say to ourselves “Did I really draw that?”

What Changes With the Right Approach

Margaret is now 65. She's completed a realistic self-portrait.

She cried when she finished it. Not because it was perfect, but because of what it proved to her.

"I didn't lose this part of myself," she said. "She was there all along. I just couldn't see her."

This transformation happens when analytical women find methodology designed for how their minds actually work.

Not occasionally. Not just with a handful of few "talented" individuals.

With consistent students who engage with systematic instruction that respects their thinking style.

The change is predictable because it's not about developing new capabilities.

It's about recognizing and directing existing ones.

When analytical women apply their existing skills to drawing with appropriate methodology, a belief shifts.

Not just "I can draw."

The deeper shift: "I AM creative. I've always been creative.

I just couldn't access it before. What else have I been wrong about myself?"

The decades-old belief dissolves.

A creative identity that was always there becomes visible.

The woman asking "Who am I without my career?" discovers: "I'm more than I knew."

Ann's Discovery

Ann Wilson told me something beautiful after completing my course:

"After studying your course, there was a significant change especially in my attitude to what I am able to learn and achieve, despite my age (now 65)."

What changed wasn't Ann's capacity. It was her understanding that her analytical mind wasn't preventing creativity—it was enabling it.

She discovered that the systematic thinking she thought made her "not creative" was actually her pathway to creative expression.

And that discovery? It changes everything.

CHAPTER FIVE

Drawing as the Carriage Home to Yourself

Yes. I teach drawing. But drawing isn't the point.

Drawing is the carriage.

What does a carriage do?

A carriage doesn't exist for itself. It exists to carry you somewhere.

It's a vehicle. A vessel. A mode of transportation that takes you from where you are to where you need to be.

And drawing? It's the carriage that carries you back to your complete identity.

Not to somewhere new. Back to somewhere you've always been but couldn't access.

Back to the integration of analytical and creative.

Back to wholeness. Back to yourself.

How I Discovered Drawing Was a Carriage

I know this is true because I've lived it.

At fourteen, I gave up drawing. I believed the myth that I just "wasn't talented enough." That lie stayed with me for nine years.

I didn't return to drawing until I was twenty-three—and only because life gave me no other choice.

I had contracted M.E. (myalgic encephalomyelitis) and had become almost totally disabled. I could only walk from my bed to my bathroom and back.

My short-term memory was gone. I had no sense of time or place. I was in constant pain.

One day, inspired by a little blue wren outside my window and my faith in Jesus, something shifted inside of me.

As I watched that little miracle of creation hopping about finding little ants on the windowsill, so filled with life, I realized that if a bird could be whole and well, so could I!

So in that moment I gathered every bit of energy I could. I decided to rise up and fight against this illness.

I set myself a goal: walk to the letterbox in my yard and back.

It took several weeks. But when I finally got there, I learned the power of goal-setting. I learned that transformation was possible, even when it seemed impossible.

But that wasn't the profound moment that changed everything.

The profound moment came after, when I asked myself: "If I can do this—if I can learn to walk again—then what else is there for me? What do I really want to do with my life?"

I cried and cried with the release.

Because suddenly I understood what was missing.

Drawing. I wanted to learn to draw so that I could fully express myself.

After that moment, I began my journey by attending a paint-on-glass workshop. It was nostalgic and reminded me to play like I did as a child. The color was incredibly healing.

More than anything I had this epiphany that I was ill because I had forgotten how to play. I'd forgotten myself. I didn't even know who I was anymore.

I was so busy trying to be perfect for everyone else and that was exhausting.

At 23 years of age, I was a qualified hairdresser and only a year and a half earlier at 21, I had just bought my first business. A hairdressing salon. I hadn't learned how to say 'no' to booking in too many clients yet, or how to delegate to my staff members.

I thought that my body was like a machine, that if my mind wanted to do it the body would just keep up.

It didn't.

After working 60 plus hours a week my body had finally given in. All of the toxic chemicals plus hard physical work took its toll.

Not only that, although I loved hairdressing, I knew that there was something missing—it was the fullness of my creative expression that hairdressing didn't quite allow me to express.

I needed a different, more permanent and more expressive medium.

The result? I'd experienced a complete body and soul shutdown of my entire body. My logical mind fatigued along with my physical body.

The M.E. was an illness that expressed itself as my body crying out for a break. A rest. Time out.

I only fully understood this once I turned to art as a form of therapy. I didn't know what I was missing before that.

There was no one to tell me that I was overworked and unbalanced in my whole lifestyle. I had no idea that balance is vital to health.

As I slowly began to heal and after that painting on glass workshop I began to branch out into other art mediums and discovered gorgeous thick luscious acrylic paint.

But here's what happened next—something I never expected.

After the realization that I truly wanted to learn to draw, I began to create amazing realistic paintings.

My drawing tool wasn't a pencil—yet. It was a brush.

The brush enabled me to create these wonderful textures that looked just like the very thing I wanted to create.

With just some "stippled" strokes using the upright brush I was painting treetops and with a few "split brush" techniques a giant waterfall.

It was a massive realization. Essentially, I could paint before I could draw with pencils.

Drawing came a little while later. It was much harder. It required creating edges, lines, and angles much more precisely. Differently.

It was just one line that had to be deeply controlled or things didn't look anything like I wanted it to.

However, for a time, I was happy painting and the images that were coming out of my brush looked exactly like a photograph. It certainly gave me a lot of attention. Everyone around me thought I was a 'Genius.'

It was mysterious to me, and I knew that something strange had happened between now and when I'd given up painting at 14 years of age. What had happened?

It took me another two decades—after working with thousands of other children and women to help them learn to draw—before I realized exactly what had happened back then.

During my hairdressing career I had developed refined comparison skills: angles, sizes, tones, and spaces.

The illness had shut down (fatigued) my logical left brain. So the voices in my head that told me I couldn't draw left me alone. With just pure painting skills, the lofty dreamy and elusive creative right brain really dominated.

I experienced that part of the right brain theory for creating images for sure. However, there was a problem.

Yes, I could copy things from pictures if I looked for long enough and hard enough and fiddled around for weeks on end, but that wasn't enough for me.

I still wasn't able to truly draw from my imagination. There was an incomplete feeling, a lack of full creative expression. I had ideas in my mind that I wanted to release onto the canvas. Therefore, I have experienced firsthand the severe limitations of "drawing only on the right creative side of the brain."

Yes, I could copy a photo. I could get a likeness in a way I never could before. But it took me months—painstaking hours and hours of struggle as I worked hard to get it right. Turning it upside down, looking in a mirror all helped a bit more, to get closer to the copied photo.

But it felt frustrating. There was no logical methodology. I had to rely on chance or hope that I'd get it right.

This wasn't good enough for me.

The worst thing about this process, though, was that I wanted something deeper. I didn't want to be restricted to just copying photographs.

I wanted to be more creative. To invent. To draw the images that were in my mind. I wanted to use my imagination and self-expression.

So I chose to rebel against realism copying from photos and dared to leave out all of the details. It was scary because I didn't know what people would say about my work. I had to do it anyway.

I began to paint in a semi-abstract hard-edge style that had a very designer quality to it. It was popular. I began to sell my work and win awards.

But I always sensed that there was more still to this whole drawing/painting mystery. Even with this abstraction style that I had invented, I still needed to "get it right." Parts of the image would annoy me, and it puzzled me. I didn't know why or how to fix the image. Again, I fiddled, I looked, I tried things.

There was still something missing. I struggled to draw some things that I really wanted to include in my art—things I had no photo references for.

They were in my imagination.

Then one day, a judge from a local art competition came to visit my home studio after I'd won an award. She gave me some valuable advice.

She explained to me that yes, my art was worthy of the prize because I had excellent "composition" and "rhythm" as well as total balance and wise color choices.

She was speaking a foreign language to me. I didn't know there were names given to the way I had placed things in my artwork and the choices I had made.

I just knew that it took me so long to try to work out the areas that felt "wrong" in my work. I had a sense of design (comparison of spaces) and knew when things weren't right but I didn’t know what it would take to fix them.

What this lady (the competition judge) told me next was absolutely life-changing. She told me there were some "rules of art" that I could learn about and use in my artworks.

She said that these rules would help me to fix the problems in my work and to be able to draw the things I wanted to draw.

For example, she explained to me about the "tangents" in this other piece of artwork sitting on my studio easel. She said that tangents were two parts of an image "kissing edges" and that was something we were to avoid. She spoke about other wonderful things that I never knew.

I didn't know that drawing was something that could be studied and learned. So that was the mysterious missing link.

After that I found an advertisement in an art magazine and enrolled in a correspondence course (yes, this is going way back to before computer days and it was by 'snail mail').

I studied the same art course that the amazing Charles M. Schulz studied (creator of the famous Snoopy, Charlie Brown and the Peanuts gang). He was my all-time hero back in the day and still is.

It took me a very long time—7 years in total, and I'd stayed well beyond my time in that course was welcome.

My instructors continued to return my marked work well after the Australian company delivering the course had stopped delivering it.

The reason it took me so long was because I struggled to understand things. I had to expand upon what was presented and practice some of the principles many times over.

I was a perfectionist and only wanted "A" grades so that meant deeply learning, practicing and re-learning as I went.

While I was going through the course I vowed and declared that upon graduation I would design a course for others that was far more "to the point" and user friendly for the deeply analytical thinker like me.

And I did.

My most famous course "The Complete Online Drawing Course" has changed the lives of more than 22,000 people and provided my bread-and -butter income earning more than a million dollars for me and my family over the past 17 years online and more income before that. It is a great course and I'm proud of it. I still offer it as well as my new course.

My most recent course is shorter, more refined and even more profound. The most powerful course yet.

It teaches retired analytical women to draw, without even feeling like you're being taught.

I'm always finding newer, easier and better ways to help people learn to draw in the shortest amount of time possible. What I thought was possible 17 years ago is radically different to what I know is true now.

Minds change, people evolve and what I discover about drawing I build into systems that evolve with time too.

The newest course "Your Creative Identity Transformation" is the result of years of research into the role the mind plays with drawing. It gets straight to the point.

We draw from our mind, not our hand. The hand is just the humble servant. So I focus on the mind when I'm coaching.

I look for the quality line, to see where her mind is at. It's easy for me to see if she's feeling stressed, impatient, lacking confidence or feeling elated, at peace.

The focus of my coaching is on her emotional processing not just the techniques.

If teaching drawing was just about teaching technique that would be easy.

Everyone would be drawing.

It's not. To learn to draw has to happen in the mind. The psyche of the person.

This is profound research. I learned this the hard way.

As I began to go deeper into the world of drawing and techniques, I began to study the rules of the great masters.

Yes my drawings improved dramatically and I was winning awards, selling my art and gaining recognition with support from the local government arts sector.

But still, something was missing.

It wasn't enough to just follow the rules. They were so helpful, but I had to have more control over the outcome of my work.

Not only that, I was fascinated about what drawing is and where it comes from. I wanted to explain this drawing mystery to others.

I realized that what was missing was deeper control over this whole creative experience.

Another huge missing link is exactly what I've since discovered and now call "the Artist's Language"—a systematic way to translate what the analytical mind sees into what the creative hand expresses.

Not just right-brain drawing. Not just copying photos or things in front of me tirelessly, mindlessly hoping and stumbling around before finally getting it right. Not just following logical (but respectfully masterful) rules.

But integrating both sides of the brain working together simultaneously. Analytical observation and creative expression. Logic and intuition. System and soul. A perfect combination of full creative freedom!

From there, I began to create my own original art fully. I learned these fundamental principles and combined them with soul. Messages from my deep subconscious were revealed onto the canvas and I learned many life-lessons through my own art.

My art healed me and helped me change the trajectory of my entire future.

I went on to become one of the city's most valued artists over a period of almost ten years. My work sold to many major corporate collections and private individuals. I won awards, government funding, and sponsorships.

I went on to set up two of the largest privately-owned ongoing art education centers in two separate states of Australia.

I learned so much about the huge benefits of learning to draw for all ages.

And after a while, I soon discovered that art—and drawing in particular—was far more powerful than I first imagined.

Drawing is a carriage that can bring about incredible healing, self-love, self-development, confidence, creativity, and so much more.

Drawing carried me from disabled and fragmented to whole and thriving. From copying photos for months to creating original imaginative work. From relying on chance to having systematic control.

From using only half my capacity to integrating both analytical and creative.

It brought me home to myself—my complete self.

So I've dedicated my life since then to help as many others as possible learn to draw as the carriage into finding the complete self.

That's why I know this works.

Not because I read it in a book or heard it from someone else.

But because drawing saved my life. Because I discovered through struggle what was missing.

Because I've lived the journey from "I'm not talented enough" to creating work that moves people.

Because I developed the methodology that finally gave me control—the Artist's Language that brings analytical and creative together.

And I've watched it transform thousands of others since.

Why Drawing Specifically?

People sometimes ask me: "Why drawing? Why not painting, or pottery, or writing? Why not sketching, doodling random shapes, or just relying on whatever comes out from the pencil onto the paper? Why do we need to truly learn to draw?"

And here's why: drawing is the most systematic, evidence-based, analytical art form that exists. It's the perfect opportunity for the delicate dance to take place between the logical reasoning part of ourselves and the creative expressive whimsical and dreamy side.

Drawing accesses the full complete person in a way that no other thing does.

Drawing is fundamental to our being. It allows us to create in a way that nothing else does.

This language between the different aspects of ourselves also allows us to tap deep into the subconscious, bringing our dreams and thoughts out onto the paper with control. When you learn to draw the things you imagine, then you can fully express yourself.

The connection you're making is deep, it's profound, and it stays with you as you go about your daily life. It's not fleeting. It isn't just "in the moment"—it's life-changing and affects your whole being.

And more than that—drawing with charcoal pencil allows for correction, adjustment, refinement. It's forgiving. It allows you to be imperfect while you're learning.

It's the ideal carriage for this journey.

Completion: Realism to Imagination

Drawing is the perfect carriage to unite us back with our natural ability to create. To be able to draw a realistic likeness is just the beginning. The training ground so to speak. It precedes the creative expressive release that comes from creating truly imaginative art.

Art from the imagination is best and most fully expressed when the rules of art are well-practiced and understood, in my opinion.

Once we've built valuable brain pathways that enable our hand to respond effortlessly to what our brain sees, then we are ready for expressing our deep subconscious thoughts through process.

Drawing enables us to create imagery that is in the subconscious, bringing it to our awareness within our mind then (because we've developed control over the drawing process) our ideas can come out through the hand as a visible image on a page.

In this way our subconscious thoughts can become conscious.

When we also include writing about our thoughts in the process, we have another level of understanding and deeper access to what lays hidden in the subconscious.

There is a three-stage process that I share with my clients who stay with me longer than the 12 week Creative Identity Transformation™ process.

I take them into the realm of doing exactly this; bringing the subconscious into the conscious through drawing as a carriage to create totally original art from imagination and referencing existing imagery where needed.

It begins with stage one:

• Heart and Soul Stage – the emotional aspect, coming up with the first inklings of an idea
• Planning Stage – The technical side of planning your artwork and choosing subjects
• Application Stage – when you finally begin your drawing

This valuable three-stage process which combines logic with intuition enables you to bring out an idea from deep within your subconscious into your conscious and then onto paper as an image.

This process can be cathartic and used as a form of self-expression and self-discovery.

The Carriage and Drawing Journey

So where does this carriage take you?

From "I can't" to "I absolutely can."

That's the surface journey. From believing you're incapable to holding undeniable proof you created yourself.

But underneath that, the journey is much deeper:

From fragmented to integrated.

For years, you've operated from half your capacity. The analytical half. Systematic, practical, evidence-based.

The creative half went dormant.

And what that created was fragmentation. Part of you was expressed, developed, used constantly. Part of you was suppressed, waiting, preserved.

Drawing carries you from fragmentation to integration.

It brings both halves together—the analytical observer and the creative expresser, working in harmony for the first time in decades.

From defined by roles to defined by wholeness.

You were the CEO. The executive. The director. The strategic leader. The project manager. The accountant. The attorney. The mother, The daughter. The consultant. The nurse. The teacher. The coordinator. The social worker. The healthcare administrator. The therapist.

Roles that told you who you were.

And when those roles no longer brought you the same satisfaction or joy, when they were completed or changed, you were left asking "Who am I now? Who am I becoming next?"

Drawing carries you to a different answer: I am a woman who is both systematic and expressive, both accomplished and still discovering, both everything I've been and everything I'm becoming.

Not a new identity. A complete one.

From dormancy to activation.

That creative capacity that's been waiting for years? Drawing wakes it up.

Gently. Systematically. Step by step, week by week, it resurfaces.

And when it does, you discover: this was here all along. I was always capable of this.

The Journey Drawing Carries You On

Through this transformation journey, drawing carries you through distinct phases:

Phase One: Foundation & Awakening

You start gently. Loose marks. Expressive movements. Permission to explore without judgment.

You're learning the medium of charcoal pencil—how it feels, how it moves, how forgiving it is. You discover how erasing and blending materials adjust your markings to become helpful additional tools to refine and explore even more.

A whole new world of fascination opens up to you when you use this raw, primitive material that is so perfect for reconnecting you back to your authentic self. Your birthright as a creative soul.

And underneath that technical learning, something else is happening: the "I can't draw" belief is starting to dissolve. The truth that you are indeed creative is slowly beginning to emerge, to peek out from behind closed doors. You are just beginning to dare to believe. At first you ask "Is it true? Is this really true?"

Because you see evidence very early on in my Creative Identity Transformation™ program, you're drawing right from the very beginning. It's hard to believe. At first it seems impossible, but then very soon you see that it IS true. You know.

Because you are drawing. Right from the beginning.

Maybe not a realistic portrait yet. But you're making marks, seeing relationships, translating observation to paper.

Then... you move into drawing real objects, creating textures and individual facial features, deeply exploring what it takes to draw general faces; the eyes, lips, nose and ears.
We are all just different. You'll see that we're actually different only by the width of a line sometimes.

Your analytical mind lights up because the systematic frameworks make sense. This is the lost language beginning to stir.

Phase Two: Skill Development & Discovery

As you slowly build, placing one block of knowledge onto another.

Progressive skill development through structured exercises.

From basic forms to complex subjects. From simple values to subtle tones. From geometric shapes to organic curves.

And you're starting to surprise yourself.

"I actually did that? That looks... real."
Confidence is building. Not false confidence or forced positivity.

But genuine confidence that comes from evidence:

I attempted this, I followed the systematic process, and I created something beyond what I thought I could.

The part of you that's been missing? She's emerging.

Phase Three: The Self-Portrait & Proof

This is where the transformation becomes undeniable.

You're creating your self-portrait. Your face. Your unique features. The proof you can hold in your hands.

And it's challenging. There are moments of doubt. Times when you feel like you actually know nothing at all, that your portrait isn't like you one little bit.

But then you remember my words: "Creating your self-portrait is a journey. At first it might look like your grandmother, mother, daughter, sister, grandchild, Aunty, or someone else.

You don't give up. You refine. You persist. You know that it's a process and it doesn't happen right away.

At first you're in the process of discovering, and with every mark you make you're understanding more about your unique face. It's a journey."

You remember to put your index finger on the exact part of the photo you're drawing. You focus on your logical questioning. Your mind is engaged and you forget that you can't draw because you just are... drawing.

You have the skills now. You understand the systematic process. You know how to observe, compare, assess, translate.

And gradually, your face appears on paper.

Not perfectly. Not like a photograph.

But recognizably, undeniably, beautifully you.

As you look into your own eyes on the page, at your nose, your lips in a way you perhaps never have, you discover the beauty that you didn't even know was there.

Age is powerful and the markings it leaves show character, hard-earned wisdom, depth and a richness of character that is totally unique to you.

You see beauty in a whole new way. You are beautiful and that in itself, is also a revolutionary moment.

Your self-portrait. Created by your own hands. With capacities you've always had. Through the soul language you're finally free to speak.

What the Carriage Delivers

At the completion of your transformation, you're holding a realistic self-portrait you created yourself.

And in that moment, everything shifts.

Not because the portrait is perfect. But because it's undeniable proof of something you believed was impossible.

You can't tell yourself "I'm not creative" anymore.

The evidence is in your hands.

Lynn Nelson captured it perfectly: "I never believed I could learn to draw. It wasn't until I created the exercise from your course of a self-portrait and that it actually looked like me that my confidence soared."

She discovered: it wasn't about being born with something. It was about being taught systematically.

The carriage carried her from "I can't" to "I absolutely can."

And once you've made that journey, you can't unknow it.

Beyond the Destination

Here's what's beautiful about this carriage: it doesn't just drop you off and leave.

The skills you learn, the integration you experience, the confidence you build—it stays with you. Forever.

Women tell me years later: "Drawing changed how I see the world. I notice beauty I never saw before. I feel more alive and complete. I'm just so much more confident now."

Because the carriage didn't just carry them to drawing ability.

It carried them to a way of being in the world that includes observation, presence, creative expression, wonder.

It carried them home to themselves.

Now it's your turn. Are you ready to invest into yourself, into a bright, bold, and exciting future? You're not defined only by your professional achievements.

You're entering into a stage of life where you can finally prioritize yourself—filled with a freedom you may not have had before.

Let me assure you. You can do this like so many other women before you. You were born with the skills to draw.

Now it's finally time to release the fullness of who you truly are and allow drawing to become YOUR carriage too.

CHAPTER SIX

Four Natural Abilities You Already Have

I really truly want you to understand how valuable this shift can be for you.

Your life can change within just a few short hours of drawing if you allow it.

Your carriage awaits. All you need to do is step into it.

To help you take those first steps towards your awaiting carriage, let me show you exactly how the capacities you developed over years of daily life translate directly to drawing.

Not theoretically. Practically.

So you can see with absolute clarity: you already have what you need.

Natural Ability One: Comparison of Angles

What you already do:

You straightened pictures on walls, they annoyed you when they were crooked. That table, it had to line up with the tiles on your kitchen floor.

One side of your suit was hanging slightly lower than the other. You straightened it. When you're parking your car, you might not get it right first time but you know when it's crooked.

This is only a small handful of comparison of angles skills in action. You've been comparing angles all of your life.

How this is drawing:

Drawing is comparing angles.

The angle of a jawline compared to vertical. Is it tilting a little bit or a lot? How much of an angle compared to vertical?

The slope of shoulders compared to horizontal. Are they level, or does one drop lower?

The tilt of a nose compared to the centerline of the face. Is it perfectly vertical, or does it lean slightly?

Every line in a drawing is an angle in relationship to something else.

And you already see angles. You already compare them. You already assess "this is tilting left" or "this is perfectly vertical."

You just do it with walls and things in your everyday life, not with pencil on paper.

The Translation:

When I show you how to draw, I'm not teaching you at all. I'm coaching you, reminding you to see angles. This is not for the first time.

I'm showing you how those angle comparisons apply to a drawing. I'm also giving you the advice on how to use your drawing tools, the instruction of various methods, and most of all the awareness so that you can make conscious what you already do unconsciously.

I'm just guiding you to awaken a skill you already have.

Natural Ability Two: Comparison of Sizes

What you already do:

When you cut a cake in half, then half again and again, you're estimating that each piece should be one-eighth of the whole.

You poured liquids, knowing that half a cup is twice as much as a quarter cup.

You compared sizes constantly: this is bigger than that by about this much.

How this is drawing:

Drawing is comparing proportions—the size relationships between different elements.

The width of one eye compared to the distance between the eyes. Are they the same, or is one wider?

The distance from the line of the eyes to the full face, is it halfway down or does the eye line sit below halfway?

The width of the face compared to its height. Is the face wider than it is tall, or the reverse?

Every accurate drawing depends on getting proportions right.

And you already understand proportion. You already compare sizes.

You already estimate "is this closer to a quarter of the way up the glass, or closer to one eighth?"

The Translation:

When I introduce you to draw proportions, you're using your comparison of sizes skills that you already have.

I'm not teaching you mathematical measurement for the first time.

I'm showing you to use your pencil as a measuring tool. To compare "the width of this to the width of that." To translate those proportional relationships to your paper.

You're simply transferring skills you already have.

Natural Ability Three: Comparison of Tones

What you already do:

You noticed when the lighting in a room changed—when the sun came out, when clouds rolled in, when evening approached.

You could tell the time of day just by the tone in the sky. You compared fabrics when choosing what to wear, knowing this shade is lighter than that shade. You compared values constantly.

You compared light and dark constantly without even realizing it: this room is darker than that room, I need to turn on a light. This fabric is lighter than that fabric.

The paint on the walls is too dark and heavy, I prefer a lighter tone to lift up the room. These are all instances where you've accessed your ability to compare tones.

The great news is that in art and drawing we have methods that you can learn that will help you further refine this skill like all other comparison skills.

How is this drawing:

Drawing is comparing tones—the relationship between light and dark.

Is this area of the face in shadow, or is it lit? How much darker is the shadow compared to the lit area?

What's the lightest light in the image? What's the darkest dark? What's the middle value?

Every form you draw is created by understanding where light hits it and where shadow falls.

And you already see tone. You already compare values. You already notice "this is darker than that."

The Translation:

When I show you how to see and draw values, I'm not teaching you to see light and dark for the first time.

I'm providing you with tools such as a value scale and methods like squinting your eyes to simplify what you see.

To compare the darkest shadow to the lightest light. To create that same relationship of tones on your paper.

You already do this. I'm just bringing your awareness to this skill so that you can adapt and use it for drawing.

Natural Ability Four: Comparison of Spaces

What you already do:

You arranged furniture in your home, understanding how pieces relate spatially to each other.

You packed your car for trips, visualizing how items fit together with space around them.

You noticed the shape of space between objects—the gap between two chairs, the opening of a doorway.

You understood negative space—the area around and between things—constantly.

How this is drawing:

Drawing is understanding spatial relationships and negative space.

The shape of space between the eyes. Is it a rectangle? A triangle? What's its exact shape?

The area between the bottom of the nose and the top of the upper lip. What shape is that space?

Every drawing is created as much by the spaces between things as by the things themselves.

And you already see space. You already understand spatial relationships. You already notice the shape of gaps and openings.

The translation:

When I bring awareness to drawing negative space, I'm not teaching you to see space for the first time.

I'm guiding you to focus on the shape of space rather than just the object. To draw the line correctly for example, that appears as the gap between the top and bottom lip—helps you to draw the lips themselves.

This one small change can make a massive difference between your drawing looking just like the person in the portrait or not.
You already have the seeing capacity. I'm just shifting your focus to include what's around and between, not just what's solid.

How These Four Work Together

Here's what's beautiful: in traditional art classes you're expected to suddenly use all four of these comparison skills at once. This is not an easy task and shouldn't be expected of anyone.

In Your Creative Identity Transformation™ I help you to first of all refine these 4 natural abilities specifically for drawing.

We use these skills by choosing one to dominate over the others before they become refined. Once refined these 4 abilities all come together naturally to work together to form the whole skill of drawing.

Learning to first of all use these four natural abilities in isolation (so that we can refine them as they become a well-developed micro-skill) is a far more sure way of learning to draw.

We use our ability to compare angles, sizes and spaces very closely together and eventually simultaneously quite rapidly (with practice) as we draw the shape of our object and the shapes of our shadows and highlights.

The skill of comparing tones is separated, added later once all of the shapes are more-or-less confirmed, they will be refined in the final stages, making the entire process logical, sequential and much easier to process.

This method of drawing gives us a logical, sequential system, making it far less overwhelming and a much more sure way to get incredible results every time.

We don't have to rely on some airy-fairy outside force to magically appear. We don't need other stimulants to help us "get in the mood" for drawing.

With my method of drawing, we can instantly get into the so-called "hidden" language of drawing. Drawing is right there for all of us.

Through using this system we don't have to "shut up" the logical brain.

To actually shut up the logical brain is a huge task. It is there to protect us and is extremely powerful.

Instead of shutting it up, we include it.

That's powerful!

Using my method of drawing with the logical brain in synergy with the creative, we can instantly shift into the incredibly beautiful feelings that come with drawing.

This method is so powerful, it's proven. It works for almost everyone who has the ability to use this type of mental processing (the ability to compare angles, sizes, tones and spaces - what I call the "Artist's Language") and the dexterity to guide the pencil.

I have helped thousands of people learn to draw with my methods over the past 3 decades.
When you draw a face:

You compare angles (is the jawline tilting?) Then you'll compare the position compared to size; is it as far as half-way? To double check you'll use your comparison of spaces skill (what's the shape of space below the jaw?

I like to name negative spaces with funny or silly things that are not the real object.

This keeps the logical brain involved, entertained and it helps to distract it from rushing us to draw symbols instead. This is a crucial step in my method.)

Only after those shapes are finalised will you move into comparing tones (is the jaw in shadow?)

The whole skill of drawing finally comes together during the shading stage where you finally refine all 4 skills using them simultaneously - rapidly one after the other and barely noticing the shift between these 4 natural comparison skills.

It feels like you're using them all at once. Integrated. Suddenly you find yourself drawing and it just feels... natural.

Exactly like you worked in your professional career—using multiple capacities simultaneously to assess, observe, make decisions. You already think this way.

I'm just showing you how to apply this integrated thinking to drawing. It's a process of breaking down the small micro skills, refining those before bringing them together as the whole skill of drawing. Just like learning to play an instrument or drive a car, learn a sport etc.

Cornelia's Realization

Cornelia Urlass from Germany told me:

"Cindy Wider as my mentor sees my drawings with her deeper understanding and many years of experience. She helps to open my eyes and to see all of the little details."

But here's what Cornelia didn't realize at first: she already saw those details. She'd been seeing them her entire life.

I just taught her to make conscious what she'd been seeing unconsciously. To apply her existing observational capacities—angle, tone, proportion, space—to drawing.

And once she learned to apply them? Her analytical mind excelled. Because she'd been using these capacities for decades.

PART THREE

The Transformation

CHAPTER SEVEN

What Gets Released When Creativity Resurfaces

Something profound happens when creativity that's been dormant for years finally has space and permission to emerge.

It's not just about learning to draw.

Something is released.

The grief that you once felt for something lost is now no longer there. A vital part of you that you were subconsciously missing is finally found. The best way I like to describe it is a feeling of "coming home" - a completeness that cannot be found any other way. A completeness that only creativity can give us.

When creativity is suppressed, a huge part of ourselves is also suppressed. When that suppression is lifted, the feeling is more than relief, it's more than liberating.

It's indescribable until you experience it for yourself.

What Freedom Feels Like

When you finally give yourself permission to release your creative self, you'll discover a huge part of you that you never knew was there.

Your hidden identity. It's an identity that was there all along and now you're just setting her free.

This is how it feels for some women, and how it felt for me when I gave myself permission to truly set my creativity free.

As the moment first dawns upon you that maybe, just maybe it IS safe to be creative, a lifelong weight lifts off.

You suddenly feel a deep sense of freedom like never before. A desire to be your true self. You knew there was something hiding all along. You didn't know what it was.

Creative expression is what it was. Now you've discovered the big secret. Yes, the secret is out. You are creative and now you're going to find that creative part of you. You're about to explore a whole new part of you.

Yes, you might feel afraid at first, but only for a very short while. Afraid of who you might become, and if others will still 'like' you or even still love you.

Then you very soon realize that it doesn't matter because this isn't about anyone else, this is for once all about you.

Freedom of creative expression is freedom of the full self.

So what does freedom feel like? It feels like permission to play, to feel deeply, to experience new things. To live more deeply in the moment—to really take time out for yourself. You don't feel so alone anymore because you realize that you're surrounded by life, beauty and love just in nature—pure existence alone.

You begin to look at the patterns in the clouds again, like perhaps you did as a child. You start to taste food more richly, and to notice the vibrancy of colors in nature. You become curious about your world and look far more carefully at details. You study the way a tiny lady beetle spreads its wings just before it prepares to fly. Can you remember doing this as a child? Maybe you'll stop to see the tiny patterns in the petals of roses and not just 'smell them.' You'll breathe more deeply, calmly and smile more.

When you give yourself permission to release creativity, you'll open up an entirely new world, a world that you only began to discover as a child before our logical world tamed you into becoming an adult. You can have both. You can be both responsible and creative, contrary to the myths that still surround us: 'starving artist loses their mind and cannot live comfortably in society...' the Van Gogh life leaves little to aspire to.

However, there is so much more to creativity than becoming an artist who is in constant turmoil. The balanced creative life is the life I live and so do many other women around the world. Women who've worked alongside me to bring out their creative self while still living a wonderful fulfilling and balanced lifestyle.

When you release your creative self through drawing as a carriage you can pick up your pencil at any time, and put it down again...at any time. It becomes a subtle part of your life, a carriage that takes you into an imaginary place for just a little while. That imaginary place feels so beautiful, calm, where there isn't a care in the world. You forget about pain, fear, problems. It recharges your 'me' tank. You go back to the real world feeling excited about life, fulfilled and balanced.

When you finally give yourself permission to discover your natural-born gift of drawing you've found your super power. Your flag of victory that you can now claim on top of the mountain of your life.

Creative release spills out into your entire life and people see you change. You're more quietly-confident. You make new boundaries, you become more naturally-confident and therefore more magnetic. You choose your lifestyle because you know that you deserve the best life has to offer. You're developing a deep self-love, self-awareness and new courage to be you.

Nothing bothers you as much. Somehow little things that once upset you—for instance about what other people think of you—no longer matter because you see the bigger picture now. They have their dramas, their pain, their lack of worth and they're simply projecting onto you. You knew this before, but now it no longer affects you. You have something far bigger, far greater happening in your own life—an incredible creative journey that you're now on. You're on a road to somewhere new, fulfilling and deeply rewarding.

Some simple things that once hurt you, now no longer matter. You're living a more peace-filled life and for those silly antics that others play with you, to hurt you, they don't belong in your life now. You're more assertive (not submissive or aggressive because you're aware that those emotions don't serve you any longer).

You become the fullness of who you are. Your shoulders are no longer stiff when you hold them back to 'stand your ground', they're more naturally poised now, with grace and more relaxed because you're not so 'wired' for battle all the time now. You know that you've won the battle already because you just are who you are and you're perfectly happy with that. You are you.

For too long you were trying to be something or someone that you thought you had to be, to survive. To please others. But that portrayal came at a price. That price was your full creative self, your deep inner yearnings of the soul, to create and express creativity from deep within you.

As you step into that arena of giving yourself permission to create, you smile. Happiness, contentment, peace is your new super power. Everyone will be wondering what you've got that they haven't. They'll say 'you look different, what's happened?'

You've won the corporate battle, you've won the relationship battles, you've won the professional battles or whatever personal battles you were going through, because they are nothing compared to the biggest battle of all. The battle you've just won was within yourself. You know deep inside that this decision to return to your long-lost creative self is actually the bravest battle of all.

And you've won. So, if you can win the battle of living a balanced, happy, fulfilled creative-led lifestyle over an imbalanced logically-led unhappy life you're a winner! This is how it feels to be truly creative, and to give yourself permission to explore, to play, to become deeply inquisitive, curious and in awe of life itself.

You'll be filled with gratitude, peace, wonder and joy because now you're living in the moment.

You're experiencing what true freedom feels like. Freedom to be the fullness of who you are.

You've woken up from the slumber, from the numbness that a logically-dominated lifestyle has given you. That false sense of happiness that you were carrying around like a ton of bricks, it no longer has power over you. You're free now, to be you. To be really, truly, deeply you and it makes you feel...happy. Content.

You're no longer living with the desire for that false sense of happiness that you knew you could never ever truly reach—that constant desire for 'more' of everything, has lifted off you. You're content now to be yourself. You don't need to be anything more. You are you and that's it.

What else changes?

The Pressure of Perfection and Fear of Failure

For decades, you've strived to be perfect.

Perfection was something you were focused on. Not in the sense of flawless. But in the sense of competent, capable, dependable.

You couldn't risk being uncertain in your career. Patients depended on you. Students needed you, family members relied upon you. Organizations required your expertise.

You had to know. You had to be right. You had to perform at a high level consistently.

And you did. For years, you rose to meet that demand.

But the pressure of that? It never fully released.

You carry the expectation: I should be good at things. I should know what I'm doing. I shouldn't struggle or fail.

And then you start drawing.

And you're terrible at it.

Your first attempts look nothing like what you intended. Lines go wrong. Proportions are off. It's frustrating, humbling, uncomfortable.

And something unexpected happens: you give yourself permission to be a beginner.
Maybe for the first time in decades.

You're not supposed to be good at this yet. You're learning. Struggling is part of the process. Imperfection is expected.

And in that permission, something releases. The pressure to be perfect. The need to already know. The expectation that you should never struggle.

It softens. It eases. It lets go.

The Voice of Self-Criticism

You know that voice. The one that's been with you so long you barely notice it anymore.

"That's not good enough."
"You should be better at this by now."
"What were you thinking? That looks terrible."

The voice that kept you striving, achieving, improving throughout your career.

The voice that's been relentless for years.

And then you're drawing, and that voice shows up immediately: "You can't draw. This looks awful. You should give up."

But here's what I share with you: that voice isn't truth. It's just noise.

And you learn to distinguish between constructive observation ("This angle is off by just a little bit, I'll adjust it, refine it") and destructive criticism ("You're terrible at this, why are you even trying?").

One is helpful. The other is just the old voice of perfectionism.

And slowly, over weeks of practice, you learn to turn down the volume on that critical voice.
Not to silence it completely. But to stop letting it run your life.

And when that happens? Energy returns.

The energy you've been using to maintain perfectionism, to defend against criticism, to prove you're good enough—it gets released. And you can use it for creating instead.

The Joy of Process

Your career was goal-oriented. Heal the patient. Teach the lesson. Complete the project.

The outcome mattered. The process was just the means to get there.

And that's appropriate for professional work. Results matter.
But drawing?

Drawing teaches you something revolutionary: the process itself is the point.

You sit down with your charcoal pencil. You observe. You make marks. You compare, assess, adjust.

Hours pass. You're completely absorbed. Time disappears.

And at the end, you look up and realize: I wasn't trying to get somewhere. I was just here, present, creating.

That state—psychologists call it flow—it's healing.

Not healing in the sense of fixing something broken. But healing in the sense of becoming whole.

You're not striving. Not achieving. Not proving.

You're just being. Present. Alive. Creating.

And in that presence, something awakens. Wonder returns. Curiosity. The joy you felt as a child when you made things just because making was magical.

That? That's a kind of joy you might not have experienced in decades.

Michelle Banister experienced this transformation profoundly. She told me:

"When I started your online course in 2020 during COVID shutdown, I never thought I would be able to draw to the level I am able to do now. I have surprised myself with what I have been able to create – and this is probably the most significant thing as it was completely unexpected after not drawing since I was at school 35+ years ago. It feels like a hidden talent has emerged – one that I did not even realise I had!"

— Michelle Banister, United Kingdom

The "I can't" belief shattered. Not slowly. Immediately.

Ann Wilson told me: "By the way, since I started drawing with Cindy, I enjoy life a lot more.

Some days I find myself waking up in the morning excited about the day because I can't wait to start or continue on that drawing."

Excitement. About the process itself.
Not about completing something or achieving a goal. About the pure joy of creating.

That's what gets released.

The Integration of Selves

For years, you've been fragmented.

The professional you: Analytical. Systematic. Competent. Focused on others.

The creative you: Dormant. Waiting. Unexpressed. Focused inward.
And never the two shall meet.

Until you start drawing.

Because drawing requires both.

Let me clarify what I mean by drawing. As a qualified art therapist, I know the true deep healing power of expressive mark-making, doodling, and therapeutic art.

These practices have genuine value for stress relief and emotional processing that can deeply address many emotional concerns and I use this process in some of my healing work.

But systematic drawing skill is different. It's about developing precise brain-hand coordination that gives you control—the ability to place onto the page exactly what you choose to create, not something random or unexpected.

This gives an opportunity to create images that represent the person, realistic object or thing we desire to draw.

Drawing with control of the process also allows us to create imagery from our imagination. This can help us to progress into a journey of true deep self-awareness through bringing the subconscious into the conscious.

Both approaches serve important purposes. What I teach here is the systematic skill that creates permanent identity transformation.

Drawing requires that you access both your analytical mind: observing, comparing, assessing, systematically building skills as well as your creative spirit: expressing, exploring, bringing something into existence that wasn't there before.

Working together. Integrated. Whole.

And when that integration happens, you discover something profound:
You're more capable than you realized.

You're not just analytical. You're not just creative.

You're both. You always have been.

You just needed the right conditions for those two aspects of yourself to work together.

And when they do? You experience yourself as complete for maybe the first time in your life.

The Ripple Effect

Here's what women tell me happens after this creative release:

"I'm more confident in all areas of my life, not just drawing."

"I'm less afraid to try new things."

"I notice beauty I never saw before."

"I feel more alive, more present, more me."
The transformation doesn't stay confined to drawing.

It ripples out.

Because when you prove to yourself that you're capable of something you believed impossible, it changes how you approach everything.

When you give yourself permission to be imperfect while learning, it changes how you relate to yourself.

When you experience the joy of creating for its own sake, it changes what you value.

When you integrate analytical and creative, it changes who you are.

Mary Egan experienced this profoundly. After her horrific car accident in 2022, she told me:

"Engaging and participating in art projects has undoubtedly helped me in my recovery.

It gave me a reason to get up in the morning. By doing this, I forgot about my aches and pains for a short period, which boosted my mood, reduced my stress and anxiety and promoted more positive emotions. My blood pressure returned to normal."

Drawing became medicine. Not metaphorically. Literally.

Because what gets released when creativity resurfaces isn't just artistic capacity.

It's vitality. Hope. Purpose. Wholeness.

What's Waiting

So what's waiting to be released in you?

I don't know specifically. Every woman's experience is unique.

But I know this: when you give dormant creativity space to emerge, when you integrate analytical and creative, when you prove to yourself that transformation is possible—something shifts.

Something that's been suppressed for years finally has room to breathe.

Something that's been waiting patiently finally has permission to exist.

Something that's been fragmented finally becomes whole.

And that? That changes everything.

When Does the Transformation Actually Happen?

The exact moment that the transformation is experienced is unique to every woman. Some women find a change takes place in her the moment she decides that she WILL learn to draw.

That's what happened to me. I committed to the journey in a single moment and from there my entire life began to shift.

Other women continue to battle self-doubt, self-criticism and carry heavy burdens from the past. The more she trusts the process and just allows herself to follow the journey with me and just draw, the sooner she experiences the benefits.

I've found that it's all about trust. When she first decides to partner with me on this journey she chooses to trust me, to guide her, to stay with her. This is why I prefer my programs to be fully coached and supported (not just sold as a self-teach course).

I want to be beside her through the journey. I am there for her, someone to talk to, to listen to her.

It's an emotional journey and over the past 17 years online I've helped thousands of women change their lives just through back and forth writing by email.

I've guided, encouraged, nurtured her through this change. A woman going through true creative identity transformation needs support. I'm there for her in my programs.

The more she leans in, to receive this beautiful process the sooner she experiences her transformation.

The most significant thing that delays the process of creative release through drawing, is avoiding to show up at the table to actually draw in the first place.

She knows when the shift has taken place because she realizes in one moment that she actually did draw that image in front of her.

It's often a series of belief shifts that occur leading up to the final moment of realization.

She first of all sees something is shifting as she explores the medium of charcoal.

Then as she creates textures, and draws some images with a likeness she begins to believe this is truly happening.

Finally when she creates individual portrait parts she sees that she can possibly draw a portrait. By the time she draws her own portrait she is ready because she knows it's just a matter of process now.

She's learned all the micro skills and she is simply integrating them.

In that moment when she proudly puts down her pencil after creating her own self-portrait, she knows.

She absolutely can draw!

CHAPTER EIGHT

The Self-Portrait That Changes Everything

You're holding a realistic self-portrait you created with your own hands.

Your face. Your features. Your unique expression.

Created by you. With skills and capacities that you didn't know you had before your Creative Identity shift.

And in that moment, everything shifts.

Why a Self-Portrait?

People sometimes ask me: "Why a self-portrait specifically? Why not a landscape or a still life?"

And here's why: because you can't dismiss yourself.

If you draw a bowl of fruit and it looks realistic, part of your mind can still say: "Well, fruit is simple. Anyone could do that."

If you draw a landscape and it's beautiful, you can think: "I probably just got lucky. I copied from a photo."

But your own face?

You studied every line, every curve, every proportion. Since beginning this portrait process, you have had to look deeply at yourself in the mirror.

You may not have done that for a long time... really looked. Maybe you found that hard at first, but as you settled into drawing you realised that all of these lines, angles and curves are you. They're an incredible record of your life.

The ups and downs, the journeys you've been on. All recorded in the emotions of your face. And when you look at your self-portrait you can see it and say "that looks like me. It might not be perfect, but that's me." There's a deep sense of self-acceptance, self-love and realisation in creating a self-portrait.

You cannot trick yourself about whether it looks like you.

Either it does, or it doesn't.

And when it does—when you look at that portrait and see yourself looking back—you can't maintain the "I'm not creative" belief anymore.

The evidence is too strong.

The Stakes

Drawing your own face is vulnerable in a way that drawing anything else isn't.

Because if you get it wrong, if the proportions are off, if it doesn't look like you—there's nowhere to hide.

It's your face. You're exposing yourself. You're attempting something that feels impossible.

And your analytical mind knows: this is the test.

This is where we find out if everything we've learned actually works.

This is where we prove whether transformation is real or just hopeful thinking.

The stakes feel enormous.

And they are.

Because this isn't just about drawing anymore. This is about identity.

Can you actually do this? Are you actually creative? Was this transformation genuine?

The self-portrait answers all of it.

The Process

Let me walk you through what actually happens as you create your self-portrait.

- **Preparation**

You don't jump straight into the self-portrait. You prepare.

You've been building skills: observation, comparison, proportion, tone, angles, space.

Now you apply all of it to human faces. Not your face yet. Practice faces.

Breaking down facial structure into geometric forms. Understanding the proportions of a generic face. Getting comfortable with the complexity.

Your analytical mind loves this. It makes sense. It's systematic.

- **Your Face Begins**

Now you start. Your face.

You take a reference photo. Good lighting. Straight-on view. Clear details. You've already done this on another portrait so you know the process.

And you begin with the foundation: the basic shape of your head. The placement of features. The fundamental structure.

It doesn't look like you yet. It's just shapes, lines, relationships.

You know the process, Cindy has taught you well. It's a matter of staying focused and just going through the process. Keep that index finger on the photo. Line the photo up so it's parallel to my drawing.

Use the Artist's Language that Cindy taught me; ask questions to do with only one comparison skill at a time...You're building the framework that everything else will rest on.

- **Adding You**

Now the details emerge.

The specific curve of your cheekbone. The exact angle of your nose. The unique shape of your eyes.

This is where it starts to become you.

And it's hard. You notice every tiny error. "That eye is too large. That nose is tilting wrong."

Your inner critic shows up: "This doesn't look like me. I'm terrible at this."

But you have guidance. Systematic correction. Evidence-based adjustment.

You remember that you're not just drawing with the charcoal pencil, the line is too thick, you use your small pen-eraser, you adjust, you mold it into shape like a sculptor who uses clay. This medium is so forgiving.

You go back and forth. It's not about getting it "right" it's about getting to know the shape, line, curve more deeply. Soon you remember all of the different parts so you refine, refine, add more black charcoal, blend with the tip of your paper stump. Erase. You're drawing with the eraser, the stump, the black and white charcoal. Not "try to feel it" or "follow your intuition."

Concrete, specific, actionable instruction.

Your analytical mind can work with that.

- **Completion**

The final phase. Refinement.

Adding the subtle tones that create dimension. The delicate values that make it three-dimensional. The final details that bring it to life.

And then... you step back.

And there you are.

Looking back at yourself from the paper.

Not perfect. Not photographic.

But undeniably, recognizably, beautifully you.

The "I Can't Believe I Did This" Moment

This is the moment every single woman experiences.

They finish. They look at their portrait.

And they say some version of: "I can't believe I did this."
Not "I can't believe this is good."

But "I can't believe I—ME—actually created this."

Because they believed they had no creative capacity whatsoever.

And now they're holding proof that they were wrong about themselves for decades.

They've awakened the soul language they thought they'd never speak.

They've found the part of themselves that's been missing.

That's not just about drawing.

That's about identity. About wholeness. About permission to finally be who they were meant to be all along.

What Shatters

In that moment, several things shatter simultaneously:

- **The "I'm Not Creative" Belief**

You can't maintain it anymore. The evidence contradicts it too strongly.

You are creative. You proved it. With your own hands.

The soul language you thought you'd never speak? You're fluent.

- **The "It's Too Late" Fear**

You learned this at 60, 65, 70. You developed new capacities. You transformed.

If it's not too late for this, what else isn't too late for?

- **The "I Need Natural Talent" Myth**

You didn't have mysterious inborn talent. You had systematic instruction and analytical natural abilities you already possessed.

Which means: what else can you learn if you're taught systematically?

The Limited Self-Concept

You thought you were just analytical. Just practical. Just one-dimensional.

But you're analytical AND creative. Systematic AND expressive.

You're more than you thought you were.

And in that moment of recognition—"I can draw! I actually CAN draw!"—everything shifts.

The part of you that's been missing? She's here. Awake. Alive. Ready.

What Emerges

As those limitations shatter, something new emerges:

- **Certainty**

Not arrogant certainty. But quiet, solid knowing.

"I am creative. This is part of who I am. I proved it."

And there's more. Along with the feelings of release come the emotions of expansion.

Where you felt you weren't "good enough" or you knew that "something was missing" that space, it's now filled with a quiet healthy self-love and confidence that no one can take away from you.

- **Expansion**

If you were wrong about this, what else might you be wrong about?

What other capacities might you have that you've never explored?

Who else might you become?

- **Integration**

The analytical and the creative, working together. Finally integrated. Finally whole.

Not fragments of a person, but a complete human being.

- **Hope**

If transformation is possible at this level, what else is possible?

What could the next twenty years hold?

Lynn's Discovery

Lynn Nelson, in her 70s, from California captured this beautifully:

"I never believed I could learn to draw. It wasn't until I created the exercise from your course of a self-portrait and that it actually looked like me that my confidence soared."

Never believed.

Not because she lacked talent. But because she'd spent a lifetime thinking she wasn't capable.

One self-portrait changed everything.

Not because it was perfect. But because it was proof—undeniable, hold-it-in-your-hands proof—that she could do what she thought was impossible.

And once you've discovered that?

You can never unknow it.

Beyond the Self-Portrait

Here's what happens after you complete the self-portrait:

You don't stop being creative.

Some women continue drawing. They illustrate children's books for grandchildren. They create portraits of family members. They simply draw because they love it.

Others don't draw much after the program. But they carry the transformation with them.

They know now: I am capable of learning. I am creative. I am more than I thought I was.

And that changes how they approach the rest of their lives.

The self-portrait isn't the end.

It's the proof that allows the real transformation to begin.

Where Six Women Went Next

Let me show you what can happen after the self-portrait awakening. These are real women who all started exactly where you are now—as complete beginners who believed they couldn't draw. The self-portrait was their turning point. But it was just the beginning of where they went.

- **Lynn: From Veterinarian to Award-Winning Artist in Her 70s**

Lynn Nelson practiced veterinary medicine for 37 years in Southern California. When she retired, she and her husband sold everything and spent eight years living on their boat, cruising from Alaska to Panama.

As a child, Lynn loved arts and crafts. In middle school, she bought a book on drawing cartoon figures.

Nothing she attempted resembled what it was supposed to, so she gave up trying.

For nearly fifty years, she didn't draw at all.

When Lynn found my course at age 70, she was apprehensive. She'd tried other drawing classes before and wasn't happy with the instruction. She thought maybe this time would be different, but she wasn't sure.

Then came the self-portrait assignment.

"I was apprehensive when we had to do a charcoal drawing of ourselves," Lynn told me. "I was blown away when I finished that the picture really looked like me. That was the point that I knew I could draw."

That moment—seeing her own face emerge from the paper, unmistakably her—shattered a belief she'd carried for over sixty years.

But here's what Lynn did next: She didn't stop. She moved from graphite to colored pencils to pastels. She started with birds, trees, rocks, and flowers. Then landscapes. Then more complex subjects that challenged her.

She created a pastel painting called "Shroud Cay" that won Best of Show at her yacht club. The same painting received Honorable Mention in the Light Space and Time Seascape competition.

Now in her mid-70s, Lynn continues to push herself. She's exploring acrylic painting. She's working on increasingly complex pieces.

"I want to keep learning and improving to see how good I can get before age-related problems show up," she said.

This is a woman who thought at 70 it was too late. Who couldn't draw a simple cartoon as a teenager. Who gave up for five decades.

The self-portrait proved she could draw. Everything that came after proved who she was becoming.

- **Johanna: The Full-Time Traveler Who Feared Failing Again**

Johanna Thebige loved to draw as a child. She took every art class she could in school. She tried self-teaching books over the years.

All were met with the same thing: failure to learn to draw the way her heart wanted to.

After high school, she married, had children, and began her career as a dog groomer. For almost 20 years, she didn't draw at all.

When Johanna and her husband decided to sell their home and travel full-time in their RV, she suddenly had time.

That deep desire to learn to draw came rushing back.

But her greatest fear when starting my course? "Yet again failing at learning to draw as I had so many times."

Every previous attempt had ended in frustration. Every book, every class, every effort. Why would this time be different?

The self-portrait changed that.

"I'm amazed at my progress since the pre-instruction drawing," Johanna said. "I never thought I'd reach the point I'm at now."

Looking at her before-and-after charcoal self-portraits side by side, the difference was undeniable. She could see it. She could hold the proof in her hands.

But Johanna didn't stop with self-portraits.

She discovered she had a gift for capturing the soul of animals, particularly pets. Her colored pencil pet portraits have something special about them—she doesn't just draw what an animal looks like, she captures who they are.

Now, traveling across America in their RV with a purpose-built art studio her husband created for her, Johanna takes commissions for pet portraits.

She's won prize ribbons at county fairs. She's built a business doing work she loves.

"I never dreamed I'd be able to sell my art," she said.

From fearing another failure to winning awards. From trying and quitting for decades to creating professional-quality work that people pay for.

The self-portrait was the moment everything changed.

What came after was discovering who she'd been meant to become all along.

- **Katya: From "Blundering in the Dark" to Art Exhibition Awards**

Katya Yanovich studied Economics in Belarus and Computer Information Systems in the United States.

She worked in IT for a financial company until her daughter was born.

Like Johanna, Katya had enjoyed drawing as a child. "The best part about those times was how easy it was to draw from imagination with complete and unrestricted freedom of expression."

But that freedom disappeared. Her actual art journey didn't begin until 2017, when she enrolled in an online drawing course. It was thrilling to reconnect with that childhood passion.

But without mentored support, she found it "difficult to stay motivated and committed." She called it "blundering in the dark"—working hard but never certain if she was actually improving.

When she finally joined my mentoring program, everything changed.

The self-portrait was transformative. Looking at her before-and-after charcoal self-portraits, the progression was stunning. "I feel like my drawing skills have improved dramatically in a relatively short span of time."

But what Katya valued most wasn't just the visible improvement. It was the elimination of that "blundering in the dark" feeling. Finally, she had expert guidance.

Finally, she could see clear progression. Finally, she wasn't alone in the process.

After the self-portrait breakthrough, Katya continued developing her skills. She moved from graphite to colored pencils. She created portraits of her daughter that captured not just likeness but emotion.

Then she created "Catharsis"—a semi-abstract piece that held deep personal meaning she discovered through the creative process.

That artwork was awarded Special Recognition in the Light Space and Time "Patterns, Textures and Forms" online exhibition.
From "blundering in the dark" to recognized in an international art exhibition.

From uncertain if she was improving to holding undeniable proof of artistic skill.

"Going from zero to being included in an Art Exhibition and receiving an award is quite a journey," Katya said.

The self-portrait showed her she could draw. Everything after showed her what else was possible when she kept going.

- **Linda: From Corporate Management to Professional Pet Portrait Artist**

Linda Elliott worked for NJ Bell/AT&T for 31 years, starting as a telephone operator and working her way up to management.

She then became a computer technician doing desktop support before transitioning to work for a special needs school system installing and maintaining their computers and network.

Like Lynn and Johanna, Linda was always drawing and doodling as a child. She took up photography and even developed and printed her own pictures. But in her fifties, something shifted. She had an urge—she wanted to paint.

She watched Bob Ross on TV. He made her feel like she could do it. She took Bob Ross classes in art stores.

She enrolled in numerous art courses, both online and in person. She was trying. She was showing up. But nothing was quite working.

Then she found systematic drawing instruction.

"I learned more in the first two weeks than all the courses I tried," Linda told me.

But her greatest fear going into it? "That I didn't have the talent to draw and I would fail."

That fear wasn't unusual. It's the fear almost every analytical woman carries: maybe talent is real, and maybe I just don't have it.

Then came the self-portrait.

Looking at Linda's before-and-after portraits side by side is stunning. The left image shows her pre-instruction drawing—the attempt of someone who believes she can't draw.

The right image, created partway through her learning journey, is completely transformed.

Realistic proportions, accurate features, skillful shading.

"When I look at that drawing to see how far I've come blows my mind," Linda said.

But here's what Linda did next: She didn't just celebrate and stop. She discovered something deeper.

She discovered she had a gift for capturing the character of pets.

Her pet portraits are precious. Cheerful. Heart-warming. They show love in their making. She doesn't just draw what an animal looks like—she captures their personality, their spirit, that special moment in time that makes them uniquely them.

Her dedication to learning has been extraordinary. She's climbed over many obstacles, walked through amazing journeys, and persisted all the way to where she is today—from one beautiful, commissioned pet portrait to another.

"I love doing pets," Linda shared. "I find it very enjoyable. I love seeing their reaction when they see the drawing of their pet for the first time. It is a very satisfying experience and happy feeling."

One of her favorite pieces is a portrait of her mother at sixteen. She gave copies to her sister and brother. They both cherish it.

Another favorite is "Puppy Love"—a large 20" x 25" colored pencil drawing of her last four dogs. This piece holds special meaning because it preserves the memory of those beloved companions.

Her commissioned work has brought joy into countless lives. One client brought home a framed portrait of Maggie, her cat, and set it on the floor. Maggie came over and sat down in front of the picture, as if to say she knew it was of her and she liked it.

That's the kind of work Linda creates—so realistic, so true to character, that even the animals recognize themselves.

When asked what happened through this transformation, Linda was clear: "Your support, patience, encouragement, gentle pushing—I have gotten to the next level."

From corporate management to professional pet portrait artist. From "I don't have the talent" to bringing happiness and joy into the lives of others through her gift of drawing their precious furry family members.

The self-portrait proved she could draw. Everything after proved she had found her calling.

- **Mary Jane: From Complete Beginner to Advanced Drawing in 15 Months**

Is it possible to truly learn to draw in about a year? Mary Jane Clark's journey proves the answer is yes—with dedication, systematic instruction, and mentored support.

When Mary Jane first came to me, she was a complete beginner. Fifteen months later, she was creating work at a professional level—work that could easily be commissioned and sold.

Her journey is a classic example of the development and growth that happens when someone absolutely dedicates themselves to systematic learning.

You can see the patience in her delicate shading and beautiful drawing skills, the care she took with every artwork, the steady building of capability.

Mary Jane started, like all beginners, with fun, easy exercises while learning fundamental skills.

She created "Peppie The Pup," learning construction drawing—mapping out foundations using shapes before adding curves last. This method is extremely valuable among professional artists, not limited to cartoon-like images but essential for realism as well.

Next came her "Silver Kettle" and "Column Fold" drawings in graphite, where she successfully demonstrated: the five major areas of light and shade correctly positioned, six levels of tone beautifully applied from white of the paper to darkest dark, three different ways of shading with soft edge, hard edge, and gradation, and blending with a stump or cotton bud.

Then the major breakthrough project: "A Shoe Well-traveled." This challenged her to combine everything she'd learned so far—texture in leather folds, the rubber sole, the laces, using methods of circling, impressing, and shading. She succeeded brilliantly.

Her portrait "Isha" in graphite demonstrated meticulous shading and long slow patience. Her outstanding skill development was now rewarding her, and all her efforts were coming together.

Moving into charcoal presented new challenges—an intuitive medium, nothing like graphite, but actually easier to get great results when you have foundation skills in shading. Mary Jane mastered it too, creating three different hairstyles, various textures like wood, and finally her own self-portrait in charcoal.

Then came perspective and proportion, where she excelled with her "Little House in the English Countryside" project.

Finally, color. With basic fundamentals solidly under her belt, Mary Jane moved into colored pencils, learning to bring together everything she'd learned and add color theory, temperature, and tone to give the illusion of form. Her "Autumn Apples on Olive Wood,"

"Purple African Daisy," and "Apple" showed stunning progression.

Because I saw enormous potential in Mary Jane very early on—her passion for drawing, her dedication, her rapid development—I invited her into my advanced mentoring level. Her "Green Eye" drawing in colored pencil on Lightfast paper demonstrated she was ready for professional-level work.

Mary Jane herself said: "When you suggested the mentor program, I was not sure it was going to be the right thing for me. I know that I would never have learned as much as I have if I had been doing this program on my own. Although drawing has been a dream of mine, I never thought I would get to this stage. You have taught me to look at things differently and to be patient with the process."

From complete beginner to advanced professional-level work in fifteen months.

Not because Mary Jane had mysterious natural talent. But because she had systematic instruction, dedicated practice, and the support to work through each stage of development progressively.

The self-portrait was her breakthrough. Everything after was discovering how far she could go when she kept building on that foundation.

- **Mary: From "I Can't Draw" to Illustrating Her Own Children's Book at 70**

Mary Egan was born in 1951 in County Galway, Ireland. She spent 37 years in nursing, eventually becoming Director of Nursing before retiring. She has three adult children and four grandchildren.

When Mary found me in 2020, she was absolutely convinced she could not and would not ever draw.

"I felt that I was not one of those gifted people born with an artist paintbrush or pencil in their hand," Mary told me. "I had a great interest in art, enjoyed painting, but lacked drawing skills."

But she was accepted into my Complete Online Drawing Course, and despite finding aspects challenging at times, she persisted. With patience, encouragement, and systematic guidance, she gradually started to improve.

She graduated from the course in November 2021.

Then she completed an acrylic painting course in October 2022.

And somewhere during our conversations, Mary mentioned something she'd been dreaming about: "I would like to write a children's book, but I would have to get someone to illustrate it for me. I don't have the confidence or skills to do it myself."

I immediately assured her: "You do have the ability. With my assistance, you will do it."

And so Mary became a mentored student. Her children's book—"Jamie and Jojo"—was born.

Her greatest fears? "Would I get bored and abandon it? Would I be unable to complete it? Where would I begin? How do I develop a storyboard? How do I draw different characters in different positions and maintain their uniqueness throughout the book? The layout, perspective, drawings, coloring—all of these uncertainties added to my fears."

Every single one of those fears was legitimate. Creating a complete illustrated children's book is an enormous undertaking, even for experienced artists.
But Mary had something more powerful than her fears: she had systematic instruction, mentored support, and a dream she refused to abandon.

Her book tells the story of Jamie, a little boy, and Jojo, a pygmy goat who was abandoned at birth by his mother. Jamie adopts Jojo as his pet, cares for him, and they have wonderful adventures together. The moral: pets and animals must be cared for in a responsible manner.

The story is set in the gorgeous green countryside of Ireland, with rolling hills dotted with adorable stylized flowers and plants. You can see Mary's love for her homeland in subtle details like the tiny shamrock symbol on Jamie's cap.

Mary created illustrations showing Jamie feeding Jojo in the kitchen, playing with him on the trampoline, coaxing him into a toy tractor trailer, Jamie's dreams featuring his beloved pet. She illustrated Mrs. Hopper hanging

clothes on the line and discovering a "wild animal" (Jojo) rolling around on her newly washed sheets. Jamie's dad sawing wood. Jojo's toys scattered about.
Each illustration is rendered in Mary's whimsical style that adds charm and warmth to this heartfelt story.

"Never in my wildest dreams did I expect to be completing my first ever children's book," Mary said. "I look back at some of the completed images and ask myself, did I really do this?"

But here's what makes Mary's story even more remarkable:

In 2022, Mary was involved in a horrific car accident. The recovery was difficult, painful, physically and emotionally exhausting.

And engaging with her art projects became medicine.

"It gave me a reason to get up in the morning," she told me. "By doing this, I forgot about my aches and pains for a short period, which boosted my mood, reduced my stress and anxiety, and promoted more positive emotions. My blood pressure returned to normal."

Drawing became literal healing. Not metaphorically. Actually healing.

At age 70, after believing her entire life she "wasn't one of those gifted people," Mary Egan is illustrating her own children's book to dedicate to her grandson Jamie.

From "I can't draw" to "Never in my wildest dreams."

From needing someone else to illustrate her ideas to creating every image herself with confidence and skill.

From a lifetime of caring for others to finally creating something beautiful that's entirely hers—a legacy for her grandchildren, proof of transformation, evidence that it's never too late.

The self-portrait showed her she could draw. The children's book showed her who she was becoming.

What These Six Women Share

Lynn, Johanna, Katya, Linda, Mary Jane, and Mary all started as complete beginners.

They all carried the "I can't draw" belief for years or decades.

They all experienced the self-portrait as the turning point—the undeniable proof that shattered old limitations.

But none of them stopped there.

The self-portrait was the beginning. The awakening. The moment they discovered: "I was wrong about myself."

What came after—the awards, the commissions, the continued growth, the joy of creating work that touches others, the professional-level skills built systematically over time, the children's book illustrated at age 70, the healing that came through creative expression—that was them answering a new question: "If I was wrong about that, what else is possible?"

That's what I see happen when the creative identity awakens.

Not just "I can draw."

But "I am more than I thought I was. And I'm excited to discover who I'm becoming next."

The Patterns I've Witnessed Across Thousands of Women

Over my 33 years of teaching, I've worked with over 22,000 people through my courses. Many of these were self-teach courses that had huge impacts—I have thousands of reviews on Udemy to prove the success of people studying independently.

But I've also personally mentored several thousand women over this time. The patterns I've noticed in who they become after are mostly evident in the change in their work, in the things they write about their journey.

The amazing thing is that I've helped thousands of women from all around the world, from many different countries, to learn to draw and discover their creative identity without having met them in person.

I can see from their mark-making the developing confidence and self-love along the way—by the commitment to excellence in their work, by the quality of mark-making and the care they put in. The words they write to me in emails express deep gratitude and awe at the skills they're developing.

I see patterns emerge in who they become AFTER. Many continue drawing and go on to win awards, create children's books, exhibit in competitions.

The most common thing I see is a deep inner confidence and peace. They no longer doubt if they will be able to learn to draw. They now know that they absolutely can.

CHAPTER NINE

Who You're Becoming

You started this journey asking: "Who am I now?"

You're ending it with a different question: "Who am I becoming?"

And that shift—from past-focused to future-focused, from loss to possibility—that's everything.

Not Who You Were

Let's be clear about something: you're not becoming the person you were years ago.

This isn't about returning to some earlier version of yourself who was creative before life demanded practicality.

You can't go backward. You wouldn't want to.

Because the woman you were at twenty-five hadn't yet developed the observational skills, the systematic thinking, the analytical precision that years of professional work gave you.

She hadn't yet learned to hold steady through crisis, to make evidence-based decisions, to see what others miss.

She was creative, yes. But she wasn't complete.

You're not becoming who you were. You're becoming who you've always been meant to be: integrated, whole, complete.

The Integration

Here's what integration actually means:

For years, you emphasized one side of yourself—the analytical, systematic, practical side.

The creative, expressive, intuitive side was less active, less obvious perhaps even hidden.

And that created an imbalance. Not wrong, exactly. But incomplete.

Now, through this transformation, both sides are active.

Analytical observation and creative expression.

Systematic thinking and intuitive knowing.
Evidence-based precision and expressive freedom.

Both. Together. Working in harmony.

That's not about balancing opposites. It's about recognizing they were never opposites at all.

They're complementary aspects of a complete human being.

And I'm certainly not saying that "if you're not creative you're not whole." I'm simply stating that to have the freedom of self-expression helps to bring together a part of you that perhaps you never knew before.

A part of you that you experienced as a child; a certain kind of freedom, happiness that slowly disappeared as you began to grow into an adult. It was left behind.

And when they're both active, when they're integrated, you experience yourself as whole in a way you've never felt before.

The Woman You're Becoming

So who is this integrated, whole woman?

She's someone who:

- **Wakes up with purpose.**

Not the external purpose of others depending on her, but internal purpose: I have something I want to create today. Something that's mine. Something that brings me joy.

- **Notices beauty everywhere.**

Her observational skills are fully active now. She sees light, shadow, proportion, relationship. The world is richer, more detailed, more beautiful than it was before.

- **Gives herself permission.**

Permission to be imperfect. Permission to learn. Permission to create for the pure joy of creating, not to achieve or prove or produce.

Permission to finally be who she wants to be.

Knows her own capacity.

She's not hoping she's creative or believing she might be capable. She knows. She has proof. She's experienced transformation.

- **Lives in possibility, not limitation.**

She asks "What else is possible?" instead of "What am I capable of?"

She wonders "Who else might I become?" instead of "Who was I?"

- **Operates from wholeness.**

She's not fragments—analytical OR creative, practical OR expressive.

She's both. Integrated. Complete.

And when she walks into a room, people feel it. That quiet power. That magnetic presence. The confidence of a woman who has awakened the part of herself that was missing and is finally, beautifully, undeniably whole.

What This Looks Like Daily

Let me show you what this integration looks like in everyday life:

Ann Wilson told me: "I enjoy life a lot more. The changes I am experiencing are gradual and subtle. It has a ripple effect on the rest of my life. Like the confidence to go out and meet others.

I am happy to join local art groups and workshops."

Notice what happened: She didn't just learn to draw. Her whole life expanded.
She's more confident.

More social.

More willing to try new things.

Because when you prove to yourself that transformation is possible in one area, it changes how you approach everything.

Mary Egan said: "Since I discovered you, I have become more aware of the beauty of the natural world.

I now stop to admire the plants, trees, birds, rivers and mountains. All of my senses have awakened."

Her senses awakened.

Not just her artistic ability. Her capacity to be present, to notice, to appreciate.

That's integration. That's wholeness.

The Creative Future

And what about your creative future specifically?

Some women continue drawing regularly. It becomes part of their daily practice.

Some illustrate children's books for grandchildren, creating legacy gifts that will last generations.

Some, like Katya Yanovich, discover they're capable of more than they imagined: "At your encouragement, I found myself entering into competitions alongside very talented and accomplished artists and having my work recognized with awards. That was quite surreal."

Some simply draw occasionally, when the mood strikes, for the pure joy of it.

And some don't draw much at all after completing the program.

But here's what they all share: they know they're creative now.
They can't unknow it. They have proof.

And that changes everything about how they see themselves and what they believe is possible.

The Twenty-Year View

You have twenty, maybe thirty or years ahead of you.

Vibrant years. Active years. Years where you have time, freedom, resources to explore who you're becoming.

What do you want those years to look like?

Do you want to spend them filling time, staying busy, finding ways to remain useful to others?

Or do you want to spend them discovering yourself, creating beauty, living from wholeness, experiencing joy in the process of being alive?

This isn't about drawing versus not drawing.

This is about how you experience your remaining years.

As someone who's winding down, declining, becoming less? Or as someone who's still growing, discovering, becoming more?

The choice is yours.

Your Answer

Remember the question you started with: "Who am I now?"

After this transformation, your answer is: "I am a woman who is both analytical and creative, both accomplished and still discovering, both everything I've been and everything I'm becoming."

"I am whole." Not perfect. Not complete in the sense of finished. But whole in the sense of integrated, alive, operating from all of who I am.

That's not a small thing.

That's the answer to an identity question that could have stayed with you for the rest of your life.

And now you know.

NEXT STEPS

Your Creative Identity Awaits

You've read the stories. You've seen the transformations. You've discovered that the "I'm not creative" belief was never true. You know the truth about drawing, where it is and where it comes from. You understand that you have all the skills you need already. Naturally. You can learn to draw right now.

So the question is: are you ready to experience this for yourself? To put this knowledge into action.

Three Pathways to Transformation

1.Begin right now today from here

This is the very beginning of your creative identity transformation. You can begin by simply knowing all of the information I've just shared with you. All of the testimonials and my best kept secrets about drawing are in this book, that you've already read.

You've already been given what is needed to begin your creative identity transformation.

To benefit from this essentially life-changing information that I've already given you, the first step is to believe this information (there is so much evidence and proof of this over on my website too at DrawPj.com) You'll find the results from years of my hard work put into the lives of so many other women there.

You'll see stories of transformations, images from before and after my program that will absolutely shock you. This is real. This can happen for you.

My top 10 tips to get you started

These are my favourite tips that will help you to begin your journey right now today.

1. Start with one simple object

Don't overwhelm yourself with complicated subjects.

Choose something simple from in your immediate environment—a coffee cup, a pencil, a lipstick.

Something that can be observed with simple shapes; square, rectangle, circle or triangle (and in the 3D form; cube, cylinder, sphere or cone.)

This isn't about creating a masterpiece. It's about beginning the conversation between your analytical mind and the object in front of you.

2. Give yourself permission to be a beginner

You haven't drawn since childhood? Perfect. You're starting fresh, without bad habits to unlearn.

Your analytical mind—the one that made you brilliant in your career—is exactly what you need now. Trust it. This systematic, logical part of you is your advantage, not your weakness.

3. How to draw-on-demand: Compare angles, sizes then spaces (tone last) not "artistic talent"

Stop looking for talent. Drawing begins with controlling the mind. It's not some mysterious unreachable , elusive thing called 'talent.'

Of course there are variations in the level of ability with drawing, that come after many years of hard-earned refined practice. Some are also born gifted with a highly-refined set of comparison skills.

Yes like a vocalist born with the refined vocals needed for unique singing. But the skill of drawing is available for all who choose to embark on the journey to learn how to access it.

Focus and engage the logical brain to immediately begin drawing-on-demand. Start looking at angles.

Which line is steeper? Which direction does this curve travel towards? Your brain already does this when you park your car, hang a picture, or arrange furniture.

You're just applying that same skill to drawing. It's not mystical. It's systematic.

Consider sizes, how long is this compared to the half-way mark, or how far down from the top is it? Consider shading and tone later.

4. Hold your pencil softly and further away from the tip

This immediately removes the pressure on your lines. It also allows you to relax and sketch rather than creating shapes and lines like you do for writing. Sketching is a more relaxed way of making marks. Smile too, it also relaxes your entire torso.

This technique can also help you to let go of "getting it perfect." There is no perfect. There are just beautiful markings to make in pencil on your page. Let the side of the tip create softer marks and stroke the page several times in the one place.

Sketch, don't try to control every stroke. This isn't about precision yet. It's about feeling the freedom of making marks on paper without judgment. You can use any graphite pencil. I love charcoal but any will do.

5. Draw for 15 minutes, not 2 hours

When you first begin to draw you don't need long stretches of time. Just 15 minutes of focused time is enough. Set a timer. Sit with your simple object. Just observe and explore the medium.

Take time to just make marks. No one needs to see this. This is just you and the paper, beginning the relationship between stroking the paper, seeing and creating.

6. Forget about "good" or "bad"

Your analytical mind wants to evaluate and judge. For now, just observe. Every mark you make is information. Every line teaches you something. There's no good or bad at this stage—only learning to see what's actually there, not what you think should be there.

7. Position your object so that you can see it well

Place your object in front of you at least an arms length or slightly more away from you and at eye level. Then begin to compare the full height to width. Do that by closing one eye to flatten the view.

Hold your pencil in your drawing hand and measure with it. Line up the tip of the pencil with the tip of the object and slide your thumb down to pinch grip the base of the full height then swing the pencil around to compare the width still pinching your pencil with the height.

Ask yourself "Is this twice as wide as the height, not quite or more than half?" Transfer your comparison of sizes findings to your paper with a lightly sketched horizontal and vertical cross.

You can continue throughout the whole drawing this way finding all angles compared to the height and width. Then add any curves last.

This is how you draw when drawing from life. Do a similar process when drawing from a photo but instead lay your pencil on the page.

Use your pencil to measure with using the same pinch grip method. Your analytical brain loves this process. It's concrete, measurable, logical. This is exactly how professional artists work—and comparing sizes and angles is a skill you already possess.

8. Start with light marks, darker later

Press gently. Leave ghost lines. You can always go darker, but you can't easily go lighter.

This removes the fear of "making a mistake." Everything is adjustable.

Everything is in progress.

You're not carving something into stone—you're having a conversation with pencil and paper. You have plenty of paper on hand. If you're using a simply pencil, use ordinary printing paper at first. Just a ream of paper.

9. Don't just perceive things - compare them

This is not just perceiving angles, sizes, tones and spaces. It's not the 'Perception of angles' I'm teaching here. I'm talking about more structure than that.

This is accessing our natural comparison skill. Whenever we compare, we always need something to compare to We're comparing angles, sizes, tones and spaces to an imaginary vertical and horizontal line.

Use a central vertical and horizontal cross and halving lines whenever possible. Draw this first onto your photograph, or imagine it as a plumb line in the air when drawing from life.

Spend approximately 80% of your time observing, comparing one of the 4 comparison skills at a time: angles, sizes, spaces, then tones last. Only 20% of your time is making marks on paper. At least when you first discover all the markings.

After that you will be released into the creative process to further refine. But always keep checking back to make sure you're not just 'making it up' and you're going off track.

Comparing requires specific questions from the Artist's Language I explained in this book. Your logical brain loves questions—so much that dopamine is released. Your questions enable you to draw. No mysterious talent needed.

It's not "seeing" you need. It's not perception or talent. To draw, you need to analyze your subject through constant comparison.

Your eyes look, but your mind does the real work. Your hand is just the humble servant recording what's in your mind, not what you try to see.

If you don't compare, your mind will "blind" you. You'll repeatedly draw learned symbols instead of what's really there. No wonder you believed you couldn't draw.

Break through the blindness. Draw from your mind using your 4 comparison skills wisely.

10. Keep your first drawing

Date it. Put it somewhere safe. Not to judge it, but to witness your own transformation. In weeks or months, you'll look back and see how far you've come.

This isn't about the quality of this first drawing—it's about the fact that you began. That you gave yourself permission. That you proved "I can."

Summary

Start here. Start now. Start with one simple object and 15 minutes.

You don't need my course to begin. You don't need my mentoring to take the first step.

You just need to trust what I've told you: Your analytical mind is your creative advantage. And you absolutely can do this.

Everything else—the deeper transformation, the realistic self-portraits, the profound identity shift—that can come later if you choose.

But the beginning? That starts right here, right now, with you and a pencil and the quiet belief: "Maybe Cindy's right. Maybe I can."

2. The 12-Week Intensive

Another option for you. This is the next step you could take if you choose to invest in yourself, with me as your guide. Your personal Creativity Coach. It's where your creative identity transformation continues on, into a new level.

Over 12 weeks, I'll personally guide you from "I can't draw" to holding a realistic self-portrait you created with your own hands. You'll learn how to access the Four Comparison Skills in a way needed for drawing a likeness to the subject. Along the way you'll naturally build the brain pathways needed. Most importantly—you'll reclaim the creative identity you set aside years ago.

What's included:

• Personal 1:1 mentorship and guidance throughout your 12-week journey
• Systematic drawing instruction designed specifically for analytical minds
• Email and video support—I'm there with you every step
• The proven pathway from beginner to confident creator
• Your self-portrait as undeniable proof

This isn't just a drawing course. This is Creative Identity Transformation™.

3. The Artist Within Legacy Program

For women ready to go even deeper and to commit to a longer length of time with me.

This comprehensive 15-month mentorship takes you beyond the self-portrait into creating truly original imaginative art.

You'll master the Three-Stage Process (Heart & Soul, Planning, Application) and create a legacy project. Some women illustrate a series of family portraits, a collection of favourite landscapes, or even begin a children's picture book for their grandchildren and other projects that are unique to her.

What's included:

- Everything in the 12-Week Intensive
- Additional 12 months of advanced creative development
- Subconscious-to-conscious creative expression training
- Legacy project creation (begin the process of a children's book, exhibition, portfolio)
- Ongoing mentorship and support

This is the complete journey to becoming who you're meant to be.

How to get started with Cindy

Book a complimentary Creative Identity Discovery Call. We'll talk about where you are, where you want to go, and which program aligns with your transformation journey.

I'll explain more about both programs and help you decide what the best course of action is for you right now.

Email me: Cindy@drawpj.com
DrawPj.com/creativity-coaching-women

Conclusion

Your Creative Future Awaits

We've come to the end of this book. But perhaps we're really at a beginning.

What You've Discovered

Through these pages, you've discovered:

That the identity question "Who am I beyond my role?" isn't a problem to fix–it's an invitation to wholeness.

That the "analytical vs. creative" false divide you've lived inside your entire life is a complete myth— "This belief kept you from reaching your full capacity"

That creative capacity you thought you never had has been dormant inside you all along, preserved since childhood, waiting for space and permission.

That the "I'm not creative" belief you've carried for decades was based on a lie–it was protective during your career, but now it's preventing your next level of transformation.

That your analytical mind isn't your creative weakness–it's your superpower, positioning you perfectly for systematic creative development.

That drawing is the soul language that carries you from fragmentation to integration, from "I can't" to undeniable proof.

That you already possess the four core capacities for drawing–angles, tones, proportions, spaces–from decades of using them every single day.

That when creativity resurfaces, something profound gets released: permission to be imperfect, joy in process, integration of analytical and creative, vitality and hope.

That the self-portrait moment–holding proof you created yourself–shatters limiting beliefs and opens possibility.

That who you're becoming is whole: analytical and creative, systematic and expressive, both everything you've been and everything you're discovering—the woman you were always meant to be.

The Question That Remains

And now one question remains:

What will you do with this knowledge?

You can close this book, return to your regular life, and let this information sit quietly in the back of your mind.

Maybe someday you'll act on it. Maybe you won't.

Or you can make a different choice.

You can decide that this is the year you answer the "Who am I?" question with certainty.

The year you prove to yourself that transformation is possible.

The year you reclaim the creative identity you set aside years ago.

The year you become whole in a deeply fulfilling creative sense.

A Deeper Explanation: What I Offer

If you're feeling called to this transformation, I want you to know what's available.

Right here, right now you can pick up your pencil and begin to learn to draw by yourself today. You can use the knowledge I've shared with you in this book. Or if you'd love some support along the way, to go deeper and learn to draw even sooner and more easily, you can choose to have my support.

The Creative Identity Transformation™ is my unique methodology. It's not a group class. It's one-to-one guidance, customized to your pace, your goals, your unique journey.

You work through systematic instruction, receiving personalized feedback on every exercise—showing you exactly where you did well, and exactly where and how to improve.

The journey moves through distinct phases: foundation and awakening, skill development and discovery, and finally creating your self-portrait—the undeniable proof that changes everything.

You'll awaken the soul language you suppressed for survival in the analytical world.

You'll discover the part of yourself that's been missing.

You'll experience the quiet power and presence that emerges when you're finally creatively whole.

Who This Is For

This transformation is specifically for:

Analytical women from caring professions—nurses, teachers, healthcare coordinators, administrators, social workers, therapists, accountants, project managers, librarians, occupational therapists—ages 60-75 and more.

Women who have carried the "I'm not creative" belief for decades but secretly yearn to create.

Women who are asking "Who am I now?" and want to discover who they're becoming, not just fill time.

Women ready to invest significantly in personal transformation.

Women who want systematic, evidence-based methodology designed for analytical minds, not "follow your intuition" instruction.

Women ready for one-to-one personal mentorship, not group classes or casual hobby instruction.

Women who are finally safe and free to explore who they never got to be while surviving in the logic-dominated world.

Who This Is NOT For

This is not for:

Women seeking casual hobby classes or social art groups.

Women who want quick results without committed practice.

Women still working full-time with limited availability.

Women who prefer group video calls over independent practice with personalized feedback.

Women not ready to invest significantly in identity transformation.

My Invitation

I've been doing this work for 33 years. I've witnessed hundreds of transformations.

And I've learned this: the women who say yes to themselves, who give themselves permission to discover who they're becoming, who take the step even though it feels vulnerable—they never regret it.

Not because they all become professional artists (though some do). But because they answer the identity question that they'd been carrying.

They prove to themselves that transformation is possible. They experience an entirely new feeling of completeness. Wholeness. For the first time in decades.

And that? That changes the trajectory of the rest of their lives.

My biggest purpose in my lifetime is to help as many other women experience this feeling as I possibly can.

But my hope extends far beyond individual transformation.

What Transformation is Possible

My biggest hope for the women who choose to walk this journey alongside me—into discovering their full creative potential through drawing as the carriage—is that their lives change significantly for the better.

That they find themselves much more fulfilled and at peace within themselves.

But even more than that, my hope is that together we make drawing important again. Deeply valued in society.

Together we can enrich the lives of future generations by sharing the truth about what drawing truly is.

No more deception about it being some elusive "talent" that only a chosen few are adorned with at birth.

My hope is that those of you who come into Creative Identity Transformation awareness will spread the word near and far. To continue on with this movement that's already started.

Let others know that they too can discover their natural gift for drawing.

Imagine if drawing became as fundamental to our lives as writing, reading, playing a musical instrument, studying science, history, philosophy, psychology. Imagine drawing as a foundation—respected and highly revered in schools and beyond.

A universal language.

Drawing used when words are not enough.

Drawing helping analytical and neurodivergent minds excel and live flourishing lives.

Through encouraging creativity and ensuring that drawing stays very much a part of our lives, together I believe we can make our world a better place.

This is bigger than one woman discovering she can draw.

This is about changing what our children and grandchildren believe is possible. We can come together and change the future. We ARE the Queen of our creative destiny and in the process, we lead others into a better, more beautiful world.

This is about ending the myth that crushed your creative spirit—so it never crushes theirs.

This is about creating a world where "I'm not creative" is recognized as the lie it always was.

And it starts with you. With your transformation. With your willingness to prove to yourself—and then show others—that creativity was never lost. It was only waiting.

So my invitation is simple:

If you're ready to discover who you're becoming...

If you're ready to awaken the soul language you've suppressed for survival...

If you're ready to find the part of yourself that's been missing...

If you're ready to prove to yourself that "I'm not creative" was never true...

If you're ready to experience integration, wholeness, the quiet power that emerges when you're finally free...

If you're ready to give yourself permission to be who you never had a chance to be...
Then this can be your year.

The year you finally answer: "Who am I now?"

With beautiful, undeniable certainty.

Then it's time.

Time to pick up a pencil and draw. Discover your creative identity transformation.

Remember, if you'd like some extra support along the way, I would be honored to guide you on that journey.

Now is the time, because if not now, when?

Frequently Asked Questions

You may have questions about whether this transformation is possible for you. Here are the questions I hear most often:

- **"I'm in my 60s/70s. Am I too old to learn to draw?"**

Absolutely not. In fact, women in their 60s and 70s often learn faster and go deeper than younger students.

Lynn Nelson was in her 70s when she began. She's now an award-winning artist whose work is exhibited professionally. Mary Egan was 70 when she started learning to draw after a car accident. She's now illustrating a children's book titled "Jamie and Jojo."

Age isn't a barrier—it's actually an advantage. You have cognitive maturity, patience, and the willingness to trust a process that younger women often lack. You're not rushing. You're not trying to prove anything to anyone. You're simply discovering who you're becoming.

And neuroplasticity—your brain's ability to form new pathways—doesn't have an expiration date. Your brain can learn to draw at 65 just as well as it could at 25. Actually better, because you bring decades of developed observation skills.

This isn't about age. It's about readiness. And if you're asking this question, you're ready.

- **"How long does it really take to see results?"**

The first shifts happen within days or even moments depending on the individual person. I've had people shed tears of release during their enrollment session with me.

The profound transformation often takes a little longer and if you go through my full program at about 12 weeks (drawing for between 1 to 3 hours per week) most women experience a significant positive breakthrough.

It's so important to understand though, everyone experiences shifts at their own unique pace. We must both enter into this sacred journey together, knowing that there is no pressure from either of us to gain a specific result. Any and all results are what they are meant to be for this time in your life.

In your first week, you'll create your first marks, your first textures. You'll see charcoal respond to your touch and start to understand the medium.

By week 3 or 4, you'll have that moment: "I can see something happening! This actually looks like what I'm trying to create."

By week 8-10, you're drawing individual facial features—eyes, noses, lips—with recognizable likeness.

Week 12 is your self-portrait completion. The moment you put down your pencil and realize: "I actually did this. I can draw."

But here's what matters more than timeline: the transformation isn't about how fast you get there. It's about the integration that happens along the way. The quiet confidence that builds. The dopamine moments when your logical brain engages. The peace you feel at your table.

Some women know something has shifted in week 1. Others don't realize the depth of transformation until week 12 when they're holding their portrait.

Each woman's journey is unique. Trust your process. The timeline will take care of itself.

- **"I've tried to learn before and failed. Why would this be different?"**

Because traditional art instruction wasn't designed for analytical minds. And that "failure" wasn't your fault.

You were probably told to "just feel it," "loosen up," "trust your intuition." For an analytical mind, those instructions create more tension, not less. You couldn't follow them because they don't make sense to how you think.

Or you tried right-brain-only drawing methods that shut down your logical thinking. But your analytical mind is powerful—it doesn't just turn off. And when you tried to force it quiet, drawing felt frustrating and wrong.

My method is completely different. I use your analytical thinking as your advantage, not your weakness. Your analytical mind is your superpower.

The Four Comparison Skills—angles, sizes, tones, spaces—are things you already do every single day. I'm just showing you how to apply them to drawing. Your systematic thinking becomes the pathway, not the obstacle.

When you ask your logical brain questions ("Which angle is steeper? How much darker is this tone?"), it gets a dopamine hit. It's thrilled to be engaged. And that makes creativity accessible on demand instead of hoping inspiration strikes.

This time will be different because you're not fighting against how you think. You're finally working with it.

- **"Do I need expensive art supplies to get started?"**

Not at all. You'll need just a small handful of items (some are optional): Black and white charcoal pencils with a good quality hand-held pencil sharpener, sketching paper and good quality drawing paper, pen eraser and a kneadable eraser. That's it.

I work predominantly with charcoal pencil in my earlier courses for women because it's forgiving. You can adjust, refine, correct.

It allows you to be imperfect while you're learning, which is exactly what you need.

Later I teach seven different mediums and five different art styles (as you move through the initial program and if you're ready to continue with me into a bespoke legacy created just for you.)

You can choose to invest in a lovely table easel if you wish, and good lighting as well as a comfortable chair, but those things are lovely additions–they're not necessary for transformation. They might come later if you choose to continue with drawing after your creative transformation.

In this course I keep the supplies simple and accessible. Quality matters, but expensive doesn't equal quality. I can guide you to affordable supplies that work beautifully.

Everything you need is either provided in my programs or easy to source with my guidance. You can start with the basics and expand later if you choose.

Some of my most accomplished students still prefer the simple setup: charcoal pencil, paper, eraser, table and your drawing course. That's all transformation requires.

- **"What if my family thinks this is silly or indulgent?"**

This is about you, not them. And here's what actually happens...

Initial skepticism is common. "Shouldn't you be doing something useful?" "Is this really how you want to spend your time?"

But here's the beautiful thing: you don't need their permission. You need your own commitment to yourself.

It's your time now, you've given out to others all these years and now at last it's time for you. If not now, when?

And watch what happens when they see your first portrait. When they realize you created that realistic likeness with your own hands.

The skepticism shifts instantly to: "You did THAT? I had no idea you could do that!"

Respect replaces doubt. Admiration replaces dismissiveness.

Your transformation changes how they see you. The quiet confidence you develop, the peace you carry, the magnetic presence that emerges when you're finally whole—people notice. They might not understand what's different, but they feel it.

And many women find their families become their biggest supporters. Grandchildren asking "Can you teach me?" Partners saying "I'm proud of you for doing this."

But even if they never fully understand, that's okay. This isn't about them. This is about you finally giving yourself permission to discover who you're becoming.

- **"Can I really learn this online without being there in person?"**

Yes. I've been teaching online for 17 years and have personally guided thousands of women from around the world—Australia, UK, United States, Canada, Europe, Asia.

I've never met most of my students in person. And the transformations are profound.

Email and video support work beautifully for this type of learning. I see your mark-making and can tell exactly what's developing—your confidence, your precision, your integration. Written feedback allows me to be detailed and specific about what you're doing well and exactly what to adjust.

Video reviews show you precisely what needs refinement in your work. And because you can review my feedback multiple times, the learning actually deepens.

Many women actually prefer this method. There's no performance pressure. No one watching over your shoulder. You work at your own pace, in your own space, in your own time.

And here's what I've discovered: the deep transformation happens in the doing, not in the watching. It's the hours you spend at your table, engaging your mind, moving your hand, building the pathways—that's where integration occurs.

My thousands of Udemy and other course reviews along with the success stories from women worldwide prove that transformation doesn't require physical presence. It requires commitment, systematic instruction, personal guidance, and your willingness to show up.

- **"What's the difference between your method and free YouTube tutorials?"**

YouTube teaches random skills. I transform identity.

On YouTube, you'll find scattered techniques, bits of information, trending tips. But there's no system. No progression. No way to know what to learn first, second, third.

And critically: there's no one seeing YOUR work. No one giving you personalized feedback on YOUR specific challenges. No one guiding YOUR unique journey.

YouTube is entertainment. It might give you information, but information without application, without feedback, without accountability—that's not transformation.

Here's what my method gives you that YouTube can't:

- Systematic progression through the Four Comparison Skills. You're not learning random techniques—you're building integrated capacity.

- Personal feedback on every exercise you complete. I see YOUR work, YOUR progress, YOUR specific areas for growth.

- Email and video support throughout your journey. You can ask questions. Get clarity. Receive encouragement when you're struggling.

- Customization to YOUR pace. Not a one-size-fits-all video you watch passively. Active, engaged learning tailored to how you develop.

- Identity transformation, not just skill acquisition. We're not just teaching you to copy—we're awakening your creative identity.

- Accountability and genuine support. Someone who knows your name, sees your journey, celebrates your progress.

Free information is available everywhere. But guided transformation? That's what changes lives.

- **"I don't have much free time. Can I still do this?"**

Yes. This is exactly why I created the Pyjama Time™ philosophy.

You don't need hours every day. You need 30-60 minutes of focused, quality time. Those small blocks you currently fritter away—that's Pyjama Time™. The morning coffee moments. The evening wind-down before bed.

And here's what's beautiful: drawing recharges you. It doesn't drain energy—it gives it back. That 30 minutes at your table with a pencil becomes the dopamine hit that carries you through your day feeling more balanced, more fulfilled, more whole.

Consistency matters more than duration. Thirty minutes to an hour every second day builds brain pathways faster than three hours once a week.

This isn't about adding another burden to your overwhelmed schedule. This is self-nurture. And when you nurture yourself, everything else flows better.

I named my platform DrawPj.com which stands for 'Draw in Your Pyjama Time™' because you don't have to wait until you're retired with endless free time (although that might be even more wonderful).

You can begin right now, in those quiet Pyjama moments when you're most yourself. Early morning as the sunrises, or at night when the sun has just gone down.

The evening meal has been all cleared away and now it’s your quiet time.

Women create time for what matters to them. And when you discover that drawing transforms how you feel, how you see yourself, how you move through the world—you'll find the time.

There may have to be a sacrifice of something else like a favourite TV program you watch, but it will be worth it.

Whatever you decide to swap for drawing will be time invested wisely into yourself.

Because it's not just drawing. It's coming home to yourself.

Acknowledgments

To the hundreds of women who have trusted me with their creative transformation over these 33 years—you have taught me as much as I've taught you.

Your courage, your vulnerability, your willingness to prove to yourselves that transformation is possible—that's what keeps me doing this work I love so much.

To every woman who has allowed me to share her story—thank you for your generosity. Your words give hope to women who are just beginning to wonder if transformation might be possible for them too.

And to you, the reader—thank you for spending these hours with me, considering whether this transformation might be for you.

Whatever you decide, I hope these pages have reminded you: you are more than you think you are. You always have been.

About The Author

Cindy Wider's life purpose is to change what the world believes about creativity and drawing.

Her biggest goal in her lifetime is to help as many women as possible experience the profound transformation that comes from reclaiming their complete creative identity.

For 33 years, she has been proving that the "I can't draw so I'm not creative" belief—the one that's crushed so many women's spirits—is completely false.

As a qualified art therapist HH Prac.(Art.Th), multi-award-winning artist, children's book illustrator, author, and Creative Identity Transformation™ Coach, Cindy has transformed the lives of over 22,000 people.

Through her internationally recognized video courses, instruction books, and transformative programs she's made her programs accessible for so many. For more than 17 years, Cindy has been the leading authority online in reconnecting accomplished professional women with the creative identity they set aside for decades of service to others.

Through her proprietary Creative Identity Transformation™ method, Cindy helps analytical women from caring and professional backgrounds move from lifelong "I can't draw" beliefs to confident creative expression—proving that systematic thinking is not a barrier to artistry, but the key to it.

She has developed methodology that respects how analytical minds actually learn while unlocking creative potential that's been dormant for decades.

She lives in Cairns, Far North Queensland, Australia, where she balances her transformational work with maintaining her own vibrant creative practice and a happily married family life.

Connect with Cindy:

Websites: DrawPj.com | CindyWider.com
Email: cindy@drawpj.com
facebook.com/CindyWiderArtist
instagram.com/cindywider/
Podcast: youtube.com/@CindyWiderArtist

www.ingramcontent.com/pod-product-compliance
Lightning Source LLC
LaVergne TN
LVHW091046080826
845145LV00002B/643
* 9 7 8 1 7 6 3 6 3 4 2 1 3 *